VICTORIES of the Heart

The Inside Story of a Pioneer Men's Group

How Men Help Each Other Change Their Lives

ROBERT MARK, PH.D.
BUDDY PORTUGAL, L.C.S.W.

ELEMENT

Rockport, Massachusetts • Shaftesbury, Dorset
Brisbane, Queensland

© 1996 Robert Mark and Buddy Portugal

First published in the USA in 1996 by
Element Books, Inc.
PO Box 830, Rockport, MA 01966

Published in Great Britain in 1996 by
Element Books Limited
Shaftesbury, Dorset SP7 8BP

Published in Australia in 1996 by
Element Books Limited for
Jacaranda Wiley Limited
33 Park Road, Milton, Brisbane 4064

Text design/composition by Paperwork, Ithaca, New York
Cover design by Liz Trovato
Printed in the United States by Edwards Bros, Inc.

Library of Congress Cataloging in Publication data available.
British Library Cataloguing in Publication data available.

ISBN 1-85230-800-1

10 9 8 7 6 5 4 3 2 1

Permissions applied for on copyright material.

What can we gain by sailing to the moon
if we are not able to cross the abyss
that separates us from ourselves?
This is the most important of all voyages
of discovery, and without it,
all the rest are not only useless, but disastrous.

Thomas Merton

With deep appreciation to all the men who have
participated in our weekends, whose stories built
this book, and to the loving memory of Dick Olney,
who is still with us on every weekend. In his words,
"Well . . . let's just see what happens."

DICK OLNEY
May 31, 1915 – October 3, 1994

CONTENTS

ACKNOWLEDGMENTS

■ **We've been blessed** to be not without each other during these past years of sorting through our own issues of being male, working with other men, and writing this book. Each of us has a truly loving and supportive friend in our wives, Carole and Layna. They have encouraged us to create weekends for men, then waited for us to return. They've listened to us hoarsely tell of our excitement about work they could only vicariously be part of. We feel their love and support.

Our children—Tara and Claire, Grant and Emily—have listened, read, encouraged, lovingly teased us along the way. Certainly, they are at the heart of why we chose to write this book. We wanted to help men take this journey into openness in order to save the children of the future. Life without Dad is not a good life. For us, life without the comfort and laughter of our children, or those we adopt when doing community service, is not a good life.

We are most grateful to our friend and editor, Lucia Valeska. Lucia took our taped meanderings and transcribed them with love. She sat with us, questioned us, helped us to extend ourselves into the material, the stories with heart and soul. Her editing helped us to identify what we've come to call "the voice." This voice has become important to us as we merged our two voices into one that carries the message of hundreds of others to you. She wrote with a heart that was one with ours. Then, painfully to us all, she became sick. We hold her close to us as she fights a battle within. We wish her well and look forward to working again on future books.

Robert Moore has been a friend and guide. We've listened closely in meeting after meeting. He stays true to a path that calls men into leadership, contribution to community, shepherding others, mentoring and, most of all, fathering. We are honored by his foreword.

There are many who have provided us counsel, feedback, support, and energy. We appreciate Jo Lief and Linda Randall, whose support helped launch this program at a time when uncertainty was strong. Later, from our core group of facilitators—Kevin Fitzpatrick, Paul Kachoris, Dick Levon, Donald Spitzer-Cohn—we learned new ideas, tested old ones, and found strength in each other's friendship. From our friend, administrator, future facilitator, and "adopted son" Neal Robinson, we got excitement, energy, challenge, and love. All our "service men" who've worked the weekends have been intimately connected to this book's evolution. Thanks guys!

As for getting this to you, Gary Shunk was the man who directed us to Element Books. Paul Cash, their editor, took on this project at a time when others were saying, "The men's movement is dead," "Men don't read," and "There'll never be a market for men's books." His enthusiasm, support, and counsel are gratefully appreciated. We wish to also acknowledge Jonathan Back's sensitive and insightful editing and the thoroughness and care of June Fritchman who greatly assisted editing the final manuscript. On the marketing side, we value relationships with the entire staff. They have made us feel welcomed and comfortable as we are guided into the public. We extend our gratitude to Del Riddle, Skye Alexander, Jennifer Collins, and the entire staff of Element Books, and to Penguin Books worldwide for distribution expertise.

FOREWORD

■ **I remember it now**—almost like it was yesterday—but it has been almost twenty-five years. My brother and I stood together in the little white frame funeral chapel at the open casket of my father. In what was almost a shriek, my brother said, "Why didn't you spend any time with me? You never would talk about what you felt, and now I'll never know." I was stunned. I knew that my father had not shared his feelings with me—but I thought that he and my older brother had had a special, more intimate relationship. At this moment it became clear to me that neither of us had really known the heart of our father. An uncle suddenly became embarrassed at my brother's "unmanly" show of emotion and tried to get him to sit down and "control himself." I take some comfort now in the memory that I loudly told my uncle to leave us alone.

My father had died of a broken heart. He felt that a re-spected mentor had betrayed him by displaying a lack of professional ethics and integrity, and he felt forced into pre-mature retirement. He had no one to talk to, and went to a doctor only when the angina pains became too much to bear. He would not . . . could not . . . speak to any of us about his pain. His "heart specialist" was a workaholic M.D. Had this "healer" been more connected with his patients, had more connection to his own heart, my father may not have died alone in the night without being connected to monitors that could have saved his life.

I write these words more than two decades later as a psychoanalyst who specializes in working with men. For most of those years I sought healing in psychotherapy and psychoanalysis for wounds that I have only recently come to understand. *Victories of the Heart* tells the stories of men in the process of healing their hearts and opening to their mature masculine connectedness and responsible empowerment. In the narrative by Bob Mark and Buddy Portugal, I found an articulate and compelling account of the larger story which is the right context for understanding my own journey of healing and empowerment as a man.

An increasing number of people today are realizing that men like my father, his mentor, and his doctor have been betrayed by a sadistic patriarchal culture which sanctions the abuse of masculine power because it has crippled the mascu-line heart. It was this same demonic cultural configuration which led us into Vietnam and which now prevents us from facing our grief—not only about Vietnam but also about the other horrors which surround us and which we are called upon to change. We now know, more than ever before, that masculine power—disconnected from the energies of love and heart—will continue to fuel the domination of our planet by monster-boys and keep us from realizing our po-tential as a species. Many have become resigned to the idea that masculine empowerment and justice are antithetical—that males are somehow beyond redemption.

Yet there is a new spirit abroad in the land. The work of The Men's Room is one of the best examples of a trend today which is international in scope and one of the few really promising sources of hope for our human future. The victories of the heart described in this volume resonate, not only with my experience, but with that of thousands of contemporary men around the world who are rediscovering the importance of reconnecting with other men and with the depths of their own hearts. Refreshed by this healing reconnection, men are beginning to be better husbands, fathers, and sons—and more impassioned and committed citizens of their communities and the world community.

Personally, I have been fortunate to know and collaborate with Bob and Buddy in their work in the Chicago Men's Network and the Metropolitan Chicago Men—organizations which seek to lead men into mature masculinity and responsible leadership. I can attest to the reader that this is not just another book. It is a manifesto coming from the heart of men of great integrity and demonstrates commitment to the healing of men, families, and communities. I hope that you, too, will find your own story in the stories told here—and that you will become a carrier of this new and healing spirit.

ROBERT L. MOORE, PH.D.
Psychoanalyst

INTRODUCTION

■ **The manuscript** is completed. With pleasure and pride we review it with our publisher's editors. Correctly, they note that there is no introduction, no guide for what is to come. We acknowledge that our urge was to enter the deep water quickly. That as readers of others' works, we've tended to skip over introductions. They've seemed at best forgettable, at worst infantalizing, as if we couldn't have figured out what each chapter was about. And yet, we cannot deny the observation of professionals that a context needs to be set. A hiker on the road of life can get from point A to point B without a map, but how much smoother, more comfortable will the journey be with a map that sets out the main roads, the sideroads, and the rest stops.

We hope you undertake the adventure of this book to discover more about your own maleness or that of one who is close to you. We want the material that follows to touch you deeply, to connect to your own story in ways that support you and the eventual telling of your story to others. From our work with thousands of men in our offices, in their corporate offices, and on weekends for men, we know that men are not from Mars. We know that men are far more than dead-beat dads, offenders, and victimizers even if these events have been part of their lives. Each of us is looking for some way to connect, to viscerally feel the goodness and wholeness of acceptance. Each of us longs for a way out of the isolation we know intimately. We are the river at its widest, looking like a still lake, yet under the surface flowing swiftly forward. To the observer on shore nothing is moving. Underneath, it is all motion.

Our fears, uncertainties, flaws, and needs that go unspoken keep us alone, competitive, disconnected from the very things that will heal us. This book tells the story of how men help each other change their lives. Through psycho-drama, guided imagery, self-disclosure, deep attention to the other, men heal the heart wounds of a lifetime that have driven them inwards. In safe, non-shaming contexts, men pour out their truths. It is not always pretty. It is often powerful. It is men communicating with the hope of acceptance, acknowledgment, love. This must begin within a community of "brothers" who care for each other's survival and betterment. From there it can be brought to the wives, siblings, parents, and others. We can bring it to others, because we have learned to be present, to listen, to be open, to release what has blocked us for years, to detoxify and depotentiate the past, and to empower the present without violence.

Men, for reasons that will unfold in the pages that follow, hold themselves up—to standards, hold themselves in—hiding, hold themselves down—avoiding disappointments, hold themselves together—fearing they will come apart, hold on—clinging to and smothering love, and hold back—from commitments that they may be incapable of giving to.

We wrote this to give men a view of themselves as experienced through the eyes and lives of other men. We wrote this to give women a new view of the depths of men's hearts and souls. Women may also learn about themselves—their similarities and differences—through their encounter with our men.

Our hope is that men will find friends, deepen relationships, and rediscover and add to the meaning of being male and "fathering." Our hope is that a bridge of understanding, respect, and friendship will be built between the genders. Keep notes on what stirs within you while reading this book. You will learn of reciprocal ways to open to others. Men, in a perfectly male way, can feel, share, nurture, love. Together we can come out of our isolation into relationship and heal the wounds of our communities.

We have tried to raise questions and guide your inner journey in a more focused way in the early parts of the book. Later, we believe you will be more self-directed, needing less support. As with any life, the beginning is the slowest, requiring the greatest nurturance. Longer strides are based on smaller steps in the beginning. Along the way, pay attention. Notice what happens within. Notice your sensations. Write them, share them. It is the safest way out of our past and into the golden dawn of our future. May your journey be healing and provide health for you and all those you join hands with.

PROLOGUE

■ **This project** really began for me in 1972 when my wife and I were both working as counselors in Toronto, Canada. I was having a terrible time with my boss, who was systematically popping the emotional blisters I had accumulated as the son of an overbearing and bitter father. The experience sent me spinning into anger and fear. I dreaded every day bouncing back and forth between feeling murderous and feeling helpless and underneath that feeling just plain robbed.

My wife caught the brunt of it as every night I re-played the day's drama whereupon I expected her to provide the requisite interpretation, support, and nurturing to balance my ordeal. She worked hard to help, but to no avail. One night she turned to me and said, "I can't help you with this stuff. What you need is a friend."

"What are you talking about?" I protested, "Are you not my friend?"

"No, I mean another guy, a man," she said. I sat back in shock.

I couldn't imagine saying this stuff to another man. In my book a man was not meant to be vulnerable anywhere but home, if indeed it was safe even there. I was beginning to wonder, as I felt the sting of my wife's suggestion that my anger was scary, if maybe a man could understand better and help me. Out there, however, it was unthinkable. Among men? No, not a good idea. Men would greet this sort of concern with a guffaw or maybe quiet contempt. A man could have a problem but unless it involved a charging rhinoceros, something big and physical, it was best kept buttoned up. Vulnerability was the preserve of women and children, the old or infirm. That was how I felt.

As time went on, however, I realized what a gift it is that my wife is a strong woman willing to speak her needs. The notion that I could talk about my underbelly self outside my marriage was an eye-opener. That's when I took the first tentative steps along a different journey. Eventually I recalled that it wasn't entirely new. There was a man with whom I had been open and safe.

As a small boy, I had often climbed up into the strong arms and ample lap of my great-grandfather Zaydee. He would say, "Tell me, Bobby, what do you know?" Looking up into those sparkling dark eyes surrounded by a mat of white hair, I laid out my wares.

"Rabbits are fast. Foxes can't catch them. I am a bad boy sometimes . . ." I went on and on with anything that popped into my head.

Zaydee would listen and nod and pat me and nod, "Yes go ahead." When I paused he would say, "Let me tell you a story, Bobby." And for hours I was transfixed by wondrous tales sung to me in a gravely voice by a huge man who smelled like candle wax and body sweat and who burst into a smile whenever he spied me coming. Magically the stories invariably came round to my own life. If something frightened or perplexed me, great-grandfather Zaydee had a story for it. Life spent as a religious scholar provided him tales for all seasons of human travail. He died at age ninety-four, when I was seven years old.

In my heart I was searching for Zaydee. In the world I was simply looking for men to whom I could open my heart as a grown man. The first leg of my journey took me through a vast desert and many years. The time when young males looked to older males for acceptance and invitation into the wisdom of the circle of men had been gone for a hundred years, leaving in its wake a pathetic exhibit of remnants: a couple of ball games, a fishing trip maybe . . . not much else.

Since the industrial revolution the life blood of relevance has slowly drained out of the connections between generations of men. Even among men who share the same time and space the connections have dwindled as the remunerated work of the world gets further from the hearth and is doled out in isolated technical specialties. (The growing number of "at-home offices" is an exception to the general historical trend and might prove ameliorative, if it doesn't further isolate these workers from the larger community.) Without pleading for a return to the past, let us be aware of what has been lost and take steps to make connections anew in this time and place.

Today there are hundreds of thousands of men who will never experience the trust, encouragement, and support of other men or the comfort and freedom of being open among men. In part, this book is an attempt to include more men in the journey. At the same time, it pays homage to the few— who come from all walks of life—who have had the opportunity and the courage to break out of their isolation. These are men who looked at their lot and acknowledged they want more. In the process they found the wisdom to face their fears and the significant rewards of sharing the agonies and joys of their lives with others.

For decades men have been labeled insensitive, uncaring, shallow in how they relate to others. But the ways men relate are the result of our history and milieu, of what we encourage and discourage in men, and how men are taught to survive. The manner in which men relate to others is often the result of early injuries and losses and some of these are absolutely unique to male socialization.

While the polarization of the sexes in recent times exacerbated the isolation men feel, it also served to uproot false notions of biology as destiny. This paved the way for profound change in relationships between men and women. Men have suffered, men feel deeply, and most men remain locked up inside of themselves. By no means does this disqualify us from intimate relationships. The task before us is to create an environment in which men are encouraged to extend emotionally without threat of derision or shame. When men are invited to the feast of intimacy and rewarded for coming out of their cocoon, lives and relationships are transformed.

This book brings hope to both men and women because it shows the beginnings of real change in our interactions with each other. In our work with thousands of men over our collective fifty years of clinical and consultative work, we've seen that men are not only capable of a range of intimate expression but that good health for men and all of their relationships requires it.

BOB ◆

ONE

Jumping In

■ **Welcome** to this book, different from others because it requires your full presence. A thousand men have passed this way and you are invited to join us. You will be traveling in the company of an unusual group of explorers whose stories will take you deep inside yourself as you encounter their work in a program known as "The Men's Room."

As you move through the terrain ahead, mark your bearings inside and out—especially sensations like your heart quickening, stomach tightening, palms growing moist, or the hair on your back prickling. Pay attention as well to your feelings—of sadness or glee, disgust, delight, anger, pride, or arousal. Whatever engages your spirit will show up first in your body.

To turn this way now, toward yourself unflinching, requires singular courage and heart. As your guides, we (and those you meet in the stories ahead) will lead you stone by stone across a rushing river into the wilderness. When you reach the far bank the first part of your journey will be done.

At your disposal, however, will be a map for the territory ahead as well as an option to travel further.

Risky Business

"A couple of regular guys, almost" is what we thought of ourselves before we got together. We were and are psychotherapists with separate private practices. In 1982 we shared a common professional perspective and had faculty positions at the Family Institute of Chicago. At the time each of us was aware of a certain isolated trudging from one client session to the next and that something was missing in our contacts with most other human beings.

In the beginning, we passed one another in hallways, occupied opposite sides of meeting rooms—basically staked out a comfortable distance apart. There were clear signs of mutual respect and interest but standing guard over the space between us was a suspicion that the other one could do some damage if he got close. There was something sacred here to protect, a foothold of sorts that no female colleague could lay claim to, but another male? Yes, he might.

One day in a supervision group on intimacy we found ourselves paired together with the instruction to tell our partner about something he/she had that we wanted for ourselves. It was an opportunity to experience what our clients feel as they search for and disclose their most private feelings. We faced each other cross-legged, close enough to smell the other's breath.

BUDDY ▼ I remember sweating. I was extraordinarily uncomfortable until I let go of the urge to perform and allowed my mind to come to rest on Bob's ample forehead, all the more imposing for the receding hairline. Reassured, I let my gaze drop into his deep brown eyes. Now it comes to me: "I want your brain," I say, "Give me your brain." The relief is instantaneous. That's the way it is in self-disclosure. I had long admired Bob's intellect and facility with language. The ease with which he navigated complexities had baffled and intimidated me.

Then an interesting thing happened as Bob took his turn. His knowing and receptive smile faded. The face shifted, pulling his features into a knot of consternation. After a pause he said, "I'm not sensing anything I want."

"How about friendship?" I encourage.

"No," he shakes his head.

"A good laugh?" I venture.

"No," he signals silently again.

"How about lunch? Or would you like my shoes?" He brushes these offers aside with the wave of a hand. In the silence that follows I watch Bob wrestle his own demons. His feelings move visibly through the body, water fills the corners of his eyes. At the last moment he sucks the tears down into a deep breath and lets go, responding rather sharply I think until I realize he is hoarse from not speaking.

"I want your hair," he croaks.

The whole room dissolves in laughter. It is a relief and so simple, this hard work. That afternoon we name the distance between us envy, and put the first risk to rest in a bear hug. We decide to take some more time together; Friday mornings 6 A.M. are all we can find, hoping to discover . . . whatever else . . . a friendship perhaps. At the time we were moving on intuition only. We didn't know, for example, that each of us suffered separately from a complete lack of authentic contact with other men. We both figured, as most do, that the loneliness we experienced was peculiarly our own. Many men suffer in this aloneness. ▼

Buddy and Bob

The events that carried us forward began with the long, sometimes uncomfortable, always intriguing process of getting to know one another. First with stories of the men in our lives, our fathers and grandfathers. Then of our shared status as the younger brother in two-child households, each with an older brother who was never close.

The process isn't easy. There is a need to surmount our own histories and much of our cultural heritage, to move past the hole left by absent fathers. A competitive instinct lurks in the wings of our awareness ready to obliterate what has been hesitantly revealed. We discover the ways we create in one another a need to win in order to protect ourselves from defeat, shame, exposure. It is as if our receptive, supportive capacities have been pushed into the recesses of our personalities, awaiting a "go" or "all clear" signal before the nurturing parts can be expressed. Opportunities arise to aid or injure and we become conscious of the choice. The discovery continues.

Eventually we are able to name our differences, celebrate the similarities, and learn to let our vulnerabilities surface where they can be examined by the two of us, rather than compressed and kept hidden by each of us in isolation. In carving out a safe nonjudgmental container to plumb the depths we retrace traits coveted in one another. To go with his perfect head of hair there is Buddy's dauntless ability to look adversity in the eye, take singular risks, challenge the incongruities—his tough and ready curiosity. There is Bob's spirited savvy, agile wit, and wizardry of perception. In all this we come to appreciate the up side of envy and, opening to its sting, we discover the missing brother.

The threads of our separate lives, our stories, families come together and emerge in a new tapestry as the relationship takes on substance and a life of its own. Like two boys playing catch, we learn to toss the ball just high enough and fast enough to cause the other to stretch without feeling the need to get even or do better or win. The winning is in the relationship and a level of intimacy we are experiencing for the first time with another adult man.

We also bring to these early meetings the turns and trials of our profession. There is in 1983 an outcry from female clients and colleagues searching for something: What is it they are not finding in men? Never mind open, meaningful, committed relationships—many of these women are looking in vain for just an honest friendship with a man. Why is expressing one's feelings, showing one cares, needing intimacy, being honest—why are these basics missing from most men's repertoire of response?

The need for closeness—some call it intimacy—in human interaction is neither quantifiable nor even visible. People who are good at it don't make more money. Yet it is essential to mental health and it is the DNA of sustaining and sustainable relationships. This precept has been noted and documented in a variety of forms by behavioral scientists for decades. In real life it goes like this. If a man or woman feels contacted, accepted, honored for who they are, they engage the world with heightened capabilities. Deprived of the essential nourishment of intimate contact with another or others, we are diminished.

(In chapter four we discuss the concept of intimacy in depth. The last two decades have seen progress. More people are able to ask for, give, and get intimacy. Yet myths persist, for example, the notion that men fear it while for women it all comes naturally.)

The challenge was put to us by the women in our lives ten years ago: Why can't you teach men how to interact intimately? This was precisely what we had worked on in our relationships. Our acknowledged hunger for authentic contact with people in our lives, especially other men, had set the stage. The initial goal then was to increase the number of men available for a new level of intimacy and a quality of relationship many are missing: (1) with each other, and (2) with wives or partners, with their children, friends, parents, colleagues.

BUDDY ▼ One morning in the spring of 1984 I arrived at our Friday breakfast meeting with a plan. Bob cut me off mid-sentence, scribbled something on a napkin, turned it face down, and motioned me to continue. I explained the concept of an experiential weekend for men—keeping the numbers small, inviting men from different age groups and backgrounds, not using last names or discussing specific lines of work. The idea was to create a safe arena where men can tell the stories of their lives in a supportive, non-judgmental environment. The dynamic should free men to open up in all the places we shut down or subdue ourselves in order to survive.

When I finished describing the plan, Bob picked up the napkin and handed it to me. It said: "The Men's Room, where men can expose themselves emotionally, where the zipper that keeps us locked up inside of ourselves can be opened." From the beginning we understood this work involved healing. By then we knew that most psycho-therapeutic healing takes place in relationship and that success is all the more likely when we recognize and utilize our relationships as healing centers in our lives. ▼

BOB ◆ Now that you've heard the beginning of Buddy and Bob, we'd like to invite you to step up to the edge of the conversation. Today we are going to begin writing the book about the last ten years of our work, about what happened next. It is a beautiful spring day in Chicago, actually, Evanston, Illinois. Buddy and I have found a quiet spot in Dawes Park and we are sprawled out on either side of a tape recorder. We'd like you to settle in here beside us as we start to work. The work always begins with a little conversation, getting in touch with our feelings about the task ahead. ◆

BUDDY ▼ At this moment I am aware of the grass underneath me. It is still a little damp and I wonder how long I will last without wanting to move to a bench. I am also aware of what looks like a monumental undertaking—starting a conversation that will turn into a book. How in the world is such a thing possible? Actually I feel a little silly or giddy as if part of me thinks we're just pretending. It is a stretch for me. What I notice now is the sensation in my chest of being excited and nervous.▼

BOB ◆ As I sit here across from you I am filled with the joy of it, the potential, the notion of letting an aspect of our history and relationship move into book form. Then too I am aware of someone listening to us, to me now, and I wonder how that person—you, the reader—feels? I'd like you to be able to tell me at what moment you become aware of . . . when you notice a sensation inside, a smile or the tear, the tightening or loosening in your chest, the sweaty palms or a nodding of your head, whatever it may be. I hope you are able to let yourself into what's happening in the story now.

Take a minute right now as you're reading and get the vision of two men sitting together on a sunny Friday afternoon and talking about their relationship, their work, things from the heart, and notice in your body and in your thoughts what kind of image comes, the sensations you may have and, knowing who you are, just notice what it is. Focus a moment on your own life path. You might jot down some reactions to what you're hearing and feeling. Do it in terms of your own life, not with judgment or criticism. Begin with, "Right now I am aware of . . ."◆

As the story continues we encourage you to consider your own story and where you are in your life. Write down whatever occurs to you. You will find it useful to keep a journal as you read. Sometimes we'll stop and suggest some exercises for you to try out. But don't wait for us. It's your story.

Hesitation: A Way of Life

BOB ◆ On the eve of Desert Storm, Buddy and I are on a flight to San Francisco to do a two-day workshop. At 32,000 feet, just before the announcement that the war has broken out in Iraq, we are reviewing underlying issues in our work with men. "There is a hesitation at the root," says Buddy out of the blue. Men hesitating to become involved in ongoing significant relationships, men hesitating period. ◆

What Makes Us Hesitate?

It used to be that between the ages of three and twelve a boy began to pretend to be a man. In simpler societies where men worked at home (farming, for example) or away from home but returning with the fruit of their labor (fish from fishing, meat from hunting), there were not only many males available for role models but ample opportunity to obtain concrete feedback on what it is to be a man—economically, socially, emotionally, and spiritually. Furthermore, the pretending-to-be-a-man stage was impacted directly by various rites of passage, rituals designed to provide a clear path to adulthood. In this way, without distraction and with a great deal of certainty, the pretending evolved into the actual donning of the robes of manhood.

This scene bears little resemblance to growing up in an age beset by rapid change in every major social institution, including the gender roles we are taught. One result is a dearth of functional, present, visible adult male role models at every stage of a boy's development. We are also missing the force and support of collectively based rituals. Some formal rites of passage still exist such as Bar Mitzvahs or Confirmations, but these are based largely on the past and do not prepare young men for today. They prepare for the ideal but not the real.

Gone too are the simple rules of community: Provide, Protect, and Share. Like the river bottom under a rushing current, the rules shift constantly so the only apparent path to manhood is to make it up as you go, to fake it and hope you make it. Consequently the developmental stage of "pretending to be a man" has grown from three years to forty-three and beyond. This is the wilderness. Into it we plunge every boy coming of age, every man once groomed for roles and behavior no longer appropriate or functional.

Suspended over this river of uncertainty everything looks precarious. Each step is taken with the fear that what you are about to do may well be wrong. This is the basis for male hesitation. The best course in this scenario often appears to be sitting still, revealing as little as possible and keeping a close watch out for the unexpected. From this position you can watch ball games, yell at the kids, balance your check book, follow the stock market, put in longer and longer hours at the office or in the gym. Or, if the frustration (from doing nothing) gets to you, you can flip a Clint Eastwood movie into the VCR and let somebody else's day get made for you.

The Sioux warrior did not have to attend seminars on how to be proactive. What was expected of him was ordained before he was born. The rules were clear, the risks calculable, and the consequences immediate and concrete. In such a setting hesitation spells death. Over here, on the other hand, hesitation is built into a "Catch-22" survival mode. To hesitate is to give us time to gather information (that keeps on changing), clear our heads (of endless input), save enough money (to handle the unpredictable), figure out the right words (to keep the request inoffensive). Out of this complexity the questions outnumber the answers and the answers are sought in isolation. A large part of our confusion and hesitation resides in the nature of contemporary life itself.

The other part of our hesitancy comes from our personal histories, from critical times when life was everything, when we were in the moment and the moment backfired.

BOB ◆ One summer when I was four years old I woke up early on a Sunday morning. Before anyone else was up I dressed quietly and slipped outside. It was breezy and sunny and the birds and chipmunks were chirping and scolding as I crept about gathering my treasures. Just as I was dragging my trucks to the sandbox, I heard the whirring sound of the hand lawnmower coming around the corner of the house. I was thrilled to find my Daddy already up and mowing the lawn. I raced up behind him and locked into pace—left, right, left, right. If he sensed my presence, he didn't let on. He kept right on going and every time he missed a blade, my pretend lawnmower cut it perfectly. Back and forth, back and forth we went making nice even rows across the yard. Grass sprayed everywhere, caking up in the cuffs of my jeans and getting in my hair. Dad marched onward in big strides but I kept up with him.

We were doing a great job together when suddenly he stopped dead in his tracks. I ran smack into him and he whirled around and stared at me. Speechless, I watched him puff up with rage. Before I could say, "Sorry," he shook his finger at me and spat out: "Stop following me. You're like everybody else, you just want something from me. Get it straight, kid. You're not gettin' squat from me. Quit looking for a handout and quit slobbering. Sissies cry!"

Just then my mother opened the screen door and called

out, "Blueberry pancakes." I sat at the kitchen table looking at a big stack of three on my plate with the blueberry
syrup running over the sides. She kept saying, "Do you
need more syrup?" and pouring it over the top. Then she
sent me to bed because she said I must be sick.

As an adult I would sooner own all the tools than ever
borrow one. I would not rely on another male for support.
Super self-reliant, I would also have made a great Indian
scout, lone survivor. Little wonder that universities and
corporations were places I consulted and my work was
private. Sometimes I rush into action ill-prepared, fearing if
I don't force myself to do something I might not do it at
all. On other occasions I hesitate until it's too late. For
much of my life I felt that close relationships with others
would hinder me. ◆

Fear of consequence is always at the base of hesitation.
Fear of failure, fear of loss, disapproval, rejection, fear of
losing face or being humiliated, fear of losing love or not
gaining it. In writing this book we vacillated between the
excitement of communicating ten years of intensive work
with men and fear of failing at the task. Together and alone
we had to work consistently to clear our spirits of the con-
tamination of fear, fear of being judged by our peers as well
as our own relentless internal judges.

Hesitation: A "What If" Equation

An important part of our work concerns decreasing the hesitations men experience all the time—hesitations that keep us
from realizing life goals, stop us from reaching out to others
and welcoming them into our lives. Behind every hesitation
is a What If question. What if something goes wrong? What
if I expose my vulnerability? What if I lose the game? What
if I tell her I need tenderness, will she find me too needy? What
if I plan a trip with my son/daughter and then I can't talk to

him/her? What if I tell my mate about an affair and she leaves me? What if I ask my boss for a raise and it makes him angry? What if I can't get it up and keep it up?

Take a moment to write down some of your own What Ifs. You may find it helpful to keep a brief catalogue of these. Some of them remain with us for all our lives, others are short term. In either case you will gain from taking a look at this quick snap shot of your obstacle field today.

When you're finished, try this exercise. Let a What If question come into your mind and feel the hesitation that follows it—the fear, anxiety, or tension. Take a minute to get familiar with your own sense of it. For example: What if I apply for a job directing another department and my boss gets angry and takes it out on me? Focus a moment on the hesitation, your fear of reprisal. Now try turning the result around to the positive like this: What if I apply for the job and my boss commends me for asserting myself, taking a risk, and having the guts and ambition to go after what I want? All of your What Ifs can also be answered by assuming the best possible outcome.

Regardless of how your supervisor might actually respond, your premonitions about the response are shaped by your past experience, by what this supervisor connects with inside you that was a part of you long before you held this job. One way to manage the fear response is to move through it to the feelings of confidence and pleasure that would accompany a rare and unexpected commendation. This is hard for all of us—men and women alike.

Every creative venture begins with a What If. Just as every What If brings us face to face with the unknown . . . always a place of foreboding and excitement. Our goal is to move through the fear into the realm of excitement and possibility, to reduce the hesitation so we are free to act in a meaningful, appropriate, and timely manner.

After this brief opening, some of you will find yourselves

easily involved and excited about the work and the stories to come. Others will remain skeptical. Certainly this is our experience inside the groups that we lead, where men withhold until something stirs deep inside them and then they let go. If you find yourself at a distance, we want to assure you this is a natural place to start. Just accept how it is. Be aware of it and move forward with your degree of reservation. This may be a What If . . . for you.

Many men have trouble getting genuinely close, becoming involved with each other beyond the superficial realm. One reason is because we really don't know what to expect. Many of us have little point of reference or comparison because we never knew our fathers. Outside of the casual bonding around sports or business deals, men are not usually given the opportunity or the encouragement to get to know one another on a deep level. In the mid-1980s the men's movement was in part a call to men to end this kind of isolation and ignorance of ourselves.

Our next step is to create a strong positive identity for men, different from anything we were taught or know. Nothing less than a new way of being male in the world. As with all creative enterprise, this one takes us willy nilly into the unknown where risks and uncertainty abound. In part it may call upon resources inside us of which we are not yet even conscious. Nonetheless, what awaits those who pioneer this new wilderness is a journey profound and exhilarating.

TWO

What Goes Around Comes Around

Come to the edge, he said
But it's too high, I said
Come to the edge, he said
Surely I will fall, I said
Come to the edge, he said.
I did. He pushed.
So we could fly!
                    — after Guillaume Apollinaire

■ **The speed** we travel is overwhelming, the demands too many, the weight of information unbearable. Feeling besieged, we numb up, tune out, blunt the awareness. But the trance we slip into to escape pain and confusion imprisons us. Believing we are victims, we succumb. In this chapter we crack the trance, make contact, enter into new relationship. Wake up. It's about breaking out.

Michael is a surgeon, forty years old, obviously overweight. He comes to the Men's Room weekend like many others: with a degree of hesitation. Not one of those saying, "When do we start?" No, Michael is thinking: Who talked me into this? What a bunch of weirdos. If I can just hold my breath long enough, I'll be out of here.

When our eyes meet unexpectedly his look says, Don't you fucking come close to me. I don't want to hear your shit about relationships or emotions . . . Get it? Since he's here, however, he focuses on enduring the weekend as reasonably as possible, all the while thinking: I don't like this. I don't like the exercises. I don't believe in this stuff. It's hokey. "Hokey" is the word he uses. Meanwhile he remains glued to the periphery. At every break he leaves the group to be off by himself.

BUDDY ▼ Halfway through the second day, Saturday, one of us approaches him. I say, "Michael, how you doin'?"

He answers, "Ummm, this isn't bad, you know? It's nice being up here . . . Lake Delavan. Nice place and it's kinda interesting."

I repeat my question. "How are *you* doing? Have you picked a shift?" (part of the work we do) Michael answers, "Well, Buddy, as you know my wife thinks I need to work on my 'isms.' You know, the eating, the drinking, the gambling. Oh, yes, and I work too much." He smiles nervously and adds, "She could be right."

Michael's words remind me of an exercise that I do myself on occasion to gain perspective. I say to him, "Michael, I want you to envision yourself at your own funeral. You're lying in the casket and your three children are just coming in the door. They're walking down the aisle now and they're taking their seats in the first row. Their heads are down and they're crying. You're dead. At forty. They're mourning the fact that the rest of their lives will be spent without their father."

Michael's brow twists. "Stay with it," I urge him, "Look

at it. Where is each child seated? What are they thinking? What's the minister saying?" Michael says nothing in response. With one eyebrow raised, he looks at me evenly for a moment and then returns to the group. He does not take another cigarette break and for the rest of the day he remains quiet. Some of the men do not speak at all. It is never required. ▼

On Sunday, we have a special session in a circle. Each man has a final chance to speak to the group. Michael walks into the center of the circle for the first time. He turns to the men and says:

When I got here I thought all of you were a bunch of shit. My opinion was that you were losers. You weren't like me, a very successful professional. You were poo poo. Then I had a vision of my three children at my own funeral. My children who know more about me than I know about them. And I heard the minister speaking of this tragic event for so young and brilliant a guy to have suffered, for his family to suffer. He spoke of how much this man has contributed to his community in his work as a medical doctor, in his support for various community causes. Tax write-offs, I heard. My children know they are tax write-offs. That's what they will be thinking because I talk about them all the time.

And this brilliant man, their father, no longer with us, they also know . . . cheats on his wife, their mother. How could they not know? They've heard the fights. I've seen the looks on their faces. All my life I've cheated. Lied, cheated, taken what did not belong to me. My feeling has been . . . is that I need to do it to you before you do it to me. I don't give a shit about anybody else. Now I'm at my own funeral . . . because I smoke, I drink, I gamble, I chase women, yeah a womanizer. I'm into pornography, that's another love of mine. When I see my children crying, I'm wondering, what are they crying for? For me? What have I given them?

Michael starts to cry. The men are transfixed. They've heard nothing from this man but polite conversation at meal times, a nod of the head in passing. They assumed him angry. He stands in their midst, sobbing. He composes himself and continues, "I love my kids. I really love them, but I don't know what to do. I don't know how to be a father. I never had a father." Everything comes out now. His stomach is flipping as he sobs, we can see it convulsing.

When a man stands to speak we say that every man stands to speak. There is a way in which every man's work is working for every man. We have been so cut off, so lacking in models for manhood and how to handle life, that each event of the weekend answers a question, fills a void. Now we turn to the others. Is there any man in this room who has these things as part of his life, who struggles with these concerns? Every man raises his hand. We all know that we are part of a legacy of avoiding, of not giving. Unless we change it, that is what we can expect back later.

Noticing . . . It Isn't All in Your Head

When we gather together a group of men to forge a new path, this is where we start . . . with the noticing. To notice means to see, hear, feel that which is around you—what's being said or being done. To notice is to become aware of what it is that's going on inside your body, where it's going on, and how it may relate to the present situation in which you find yourself. So we start with the noticing and we start with our bodies as these are the homes of our psyches and souls.

Howard is talking about his family. Every time he mentions his children his right hand flies up to his chest. Just as quickly he removes it. We interrupt this pattern and ask him to place his hand back on his chest. We ask him to tell us about the sensation that keeps pulling it up there. With that, Howard's eyes fill with tears. "Howard," we ask, "what would the tears say if they could speak?" He says they would say, "I miss my children."

Tuning into this dialogue between body and psyche requires focus and sensitivity to the signals sent and received. Think of the body as a lie detector as well as the springboard for all emotions. It reacts in nanoseconds to every experience we have. When we're willing to listen, it gives us access to our feelings. It never lies; it is our best ally. Yet often we leave it in a heap, ignoring this fabulous reservoir of intelligence and information. Nothing sent out, nothing received.

Body Talk

Noticing body sensation takes practice. The words that communicate them come later. Sometimes the body's message is loud and clear enough to elicit tears or heart palpitations. Other times it speaks subtly. The sensations may include a tightening of the jaw and neck muscles, stomach flutters, an opening sensation, or a dryness signaled by the urge to wet the lips. We have blocked the flow of information between the body and mind so long that only the strongest sensations break through.

With practice the sensation and feelings become conscious as you learn to connect them to current or past experience. The next time you get angry or frustrated, notice where it surfaces in your body. Does it go to the neck or shoulders or the middle of the back? Is there a tightening in the chest, or is it like a walnut in the solar plexus? If your body wants to cry, let it be. Tears cleanse the wound remembered and celebrate the joy that runs deep inside you. This is how a man begins to heal himself, to explore and honor his private life process.

Charles is twenty-nine years old, a former active-duty Marine still in the reserves. Every inch of him looks like Marine—steady, tough, all muscle from the brow down. As the second day of the weekend unfolds, Charles begins to pace off the perimeter of an imaginary triangle he has cut out for himself at one end of the room. He takes in the action in the center of the room, and then breaks away to pace. Resumes watching, then pacing. The tension in him is building. As the day wears on, the speed of pace picks up. Finally everyone notices. He is the kind of guy you think twice about approaching. You can feel the energy spilling off of him, filling the room.

By 7 P.M. Saturday evening many men have stepped into the center to speak their hearts and minds. As one man finishes, Charles comes forward. He opens softly . . . stating that he is an alcoholic, the son of an alcoholic mother and a father who turned tail and ran in effect. Although Charles and his mother have been in treatment for a number of years, he still looks for relief from an agony he carries. "I have a blackness inside of me," he says, cupping his hands against his lower abdomen. At the center of his being he describes a mass of sticky black, pitch, tar, gunk. He can feel it.

He speaks of being a boy, of watching his mother begin to drink in the afternoon, trying to stop her, failing. She falls asleep at the dinner table. His father, a high-powered attorney, leaves the house at the crack of dawn and doesn't return until dinner. At the table, with his wife slumped over at the other end, his five children looking on anxiously, he casts his eyes downward and eats in silence. He spends as much time as possible away from home. Charles continues:

> I have an older sister. The rest of the kids are younger. Mother stumbles through the house at 3 A.M. shouting, Get up, get up, it's time to get ready for school! I call to her, Ma, we don't have to be at school until nine o'clock in the morning. You need to get ready! she shouts back, utterly disoriented. When I get home from school she's halfway through a fifth of Seagrams V.O. Every day she polishes off a fifth of Seagrams V.O. Every day she greets me the same. My father's job is to replenish it.
>
> I say to him: Dad, you've got to do something about

Mom. It's dangerous for the little kids. And he answers, I can't do anything. I don't know what to do. I can't leave her. I'll come home earlier. He never does. He is as scared as I am. I watch out for the others, make sure they have clean clothes, food, baths, do their homework, get to the doctor, everything. I don't hate her. I love her. It tears me up.

BOB ◆ Buddy steps into the circle with Charles and I focus on the others. The men spread out now so that we are about ten or fifteen feet apart and the same distance from Buddy and Charles in the center. "Charles," Buddy asks, "this blackness . . . where exactly does it start?" Charles points to his lower abdomen. Buddy holds up a thumb and says, "I'm going to put my thumb on the lowest part of this blackness. I want to see if we can raise it up through the center of your body. And I want you to make a noise as it moves."

He puts one arm behind Charles and uses that hand to push from the back, while his thumb plunges deep into Charles' body at the point he had indicated. We see Buddy's fist disappear into this man's stomach. Charles nods and gasps, "Yeah, that's it." Then he throws back his head and lets out a thirty-second-long shriek. A soul wrenching, ear splitting shriek, with his tongue sticking out. Buddy shouts: "Again!" And with that he thrusts his thumb into the same place. Charles throws his head back and lets out an unearthly howl . . . then buckles forward into Buddy's arms. ◆

BUDDY ▼ I let him lay his head on my shoulder and tell him, "Breathe, take it easy." Then I say, "Are you ready?" Now I'm going to take the thumb and see how far this black gunk has moved. I poke my thumb up four or five spaces. When I'm right underneath the solar plexus, Charles says, "That's it. Right there!"

It has traveled upward. This is a block, a real block. A lump of tar. It has gone up about four inches. "Are you ready?" I shout to Charles. "Yes", he says. Once again I put my arm around him to push from the back while I thrust my thumb into the center of a spot right beneath the solar plexus. ▼

BOB ◆ Meanwhile, Charles has turned deep purple while four or five guys around the circle have gone white. Three or four others are saying, "No, no, I don't believe this." They are afraid Buddy is going to hurt him. One guy has started to cry and I signal to a service man to put his arm around him. Rosemary's Baby . . . is what I'm thinking . . . when Buddy goes into the solar plexus. ◆

BUDDY ▼ The shriek shakes the room as if the devil himself were roused from hell. This eight-year-old boy who never before got his rage out, who has spent years soaking his emotions in alcohol to keep it down, is just now throwing it up. Not literally, but letting me help him move it up. I continue. It has to be two or three minutes . . . a long time to push into someone's stomach. I am using all my strength. All the while Charles is moaning, "Oh, ow, ow!" Sweat pouring off him, he shrieks again. ▼

BOB ◆ Buddy is bathed in sweat. Charles is bathed in sweat as he rests again with his head on Buddy's shoulder. We've got men around who are chalk white. They're going right through it with him. And again Buddy is shouting, "Are you ready?" Charles moans "Yes." And on it goes. Men everywhere are shaking their heads, No. ◆

BUDDY ▼ Very slowly I take it up, move it up to about the breast bone. "Yeah," he says, "It's right there." I go in again, as hard as I can into his breast bone. His head pops back and out comes the shriek—shrill, bone-chilling. I'm looking at him, making sure he's okay. He has surrendered to the process, totally surrendered. He's limp. His hands and arms are down. He just throws his head back and lets the sound from the rib cage come forth. ▼

BOB ◆ Men are shaking. Half a dozen of them have service men with them (previous participants who return to assist) because they're weak from watching. Next Buddy moves up from the breast bone to the bottom of the throat. Charles is ready, raising his chin slightly to accommodate the next jab. With his thumb Buddy goes right into the throat. Charles' head jerks back and the shriek comes.

It's like watching a man being bayoneted in the throat. That was the image that several of us got. Men are having to look away. This man is working for all of us. For all of us . . . getting up the darkness inside of all of us. The veins in Charles' neck are bulging, his tendons twitching with emotion that keeps coming up. ◆

BUDDY ▼ The shriek lasts a minute and a half and he collapses against my shoulder. He's sopping wet but wants to go on. He points past the Adam's apple, above it, right before the chin, under the tongue. We do it again. This time he can't get out a scream. It's a gurgling sound as if he were in pain but has to keep the volume down . . . It goes on and on. ▼

BOB ◆ It's a death rattle. Every man in the room has sunk to his knees. The circle has closed around Buddy and Charles. We can almost touch them. We have been at this exercise for twenty minutes . . . and we go again. With one finger Charles touches a point on his lower jaw, just under the lip.

I figure . . . it's stitches. He's going to need six stitches.

Whatever is moving up through his body, the thing is going to explode in blood. Buddy puts one hand behind Charles' head and with his finger starts into the lower gum where Charles is pointing. The color has left the room. It is white and it is black. And then, amazingly, it's over. ◆

BUDDY ▼ I give the final push, Charles spits, and it's out. Now I take my thumb and I go back to the original spot in his lower abdomen. I move up slowly, pushing in a line straight up through his whole body. All the way up. Charles whispers, "That's it. It's done."

He stands up straight and looks at each man around the circle. He has not looked at the others until now. Every man is peaked, rapt, and spent at the same time by the catharsis shared. There are thirty men with whom Charles has connected. They have taken in the battle, tasted it, are bound by it. Their eyes meet his in wonder and in thanks for the work done . . . for all of us. Any doubt that the body takes, holds, and can yield up experience is gone.

One man walks up to Charles declaring exuberantly, "I'm so proud of you. I would have you be my son or son-in-law." And Charles says, "You have daughters?" The man declares proudly "Yes, I have two daughters!" And Charles says, "They're available?" The man says, "Oh no, they're both married." Charles responds, "You mean I went through this for nothing?" Everyone laughs. The relief is palpable. There is amazing grace in this work, a kind of resurrection occurs by the time it is done.

But you have to realize what it means and what it doesn't. The catharsis is a beginning, not an end. Later on, Charles stands to speak these words: "I am my mother's son. I am alcoholic. I am abusive to others. I withdraw. I don't know if I really want to be healthy. The choice is mine."

This is the work. Do we choose to continue to act out of early pain or do we choose another way and for what

reason? The purpose of the catharsis is solely to understand that a choice is possible. Up until then you don't
know if you can or you can't. It has you.

Several days after the weekend, Charles stops by my office to relate the following. "The moment I spit the stuff
out my mouth . . . I couldn't say anything then . . . four
white, cloud-like circles appeared in the air in front of
me. As I discharged this black substance it filled the circles
one at a time. Then, whoosh! The four clouds took off, disappearing in the distance." ▼

Some of us spontaneously move to a sensual, in this case
visual, plane upon emotional impact. This kind of imaging is
an important implement in all healing process. The tendency is to censor unexpected images that arrive to symbol-
ize a change taking place inside of us. Charles kept this one.
The image of this mass of despair carried off by white clouds
serves to remind him and us of what is possible. Until then,
Charles was merely a re-enactment of what had been handed
down to him. With his work and this image, he could begin
to move along a different path.

Biology and Culture Vie for a Voice

Women are attuned to the body through biological remind-
ers such as menstruation, childbirth, lactation, and menopause. For them the link between body and emotions is a
routine experience. Because men are without these remind-
ers, because Euro-western tradition does not honor the body/
mind connection, and because male socialization in our
culture favors screening out feelings, many men remain
unaware that their own bodies speak to them every day.

Some theorists believe that young boys are initially turned
away from their bodies around the age of three, when they
are directed by parents, other adults, older children, and me-
dia to emulate and join their male role models—role models

who are often distant, less nurturing than previous female role models and sometimes even feared. In such cases a tremendous loss happens without the language to deal with it. A resistance develops where bodily sensations associated with emotions are blocked, as shown by Michael Franz Basch, M.D. The loss here has to do with a break in intimate connection, that is, the loss of a knowing contact with the adult in charge. This loss will be experienced again in many different forms and settings as boy becomes man. Boys nurtured from infancy by an adult male might well grow up with the connection between emotions and body sensation intact. In any case, what is done is done. We must not languish in what wasn't or was for us. No matter what the early experiences taught, there is only one place to move into now.

Presence of Heart

Living in the past, we can dwell on what might have been. Living in the future, we can dwell on what we wish for. But only in the present can we take charge of the moment. Many of us trudge along with about a 20 to 25 percent presence. We're conscious enough to be able to drive, to carry on a basic conversation, to get our work done at some reasonable level. But we're not present in the sense of bringing our actual ability, our full consciousness, our whole energy capacity to our work or into our relationships.

The notion of a full presence, and the vital role it plays in mental health, inspired the birth of a school of psychology in the late 1940s. Those of you who are familiar with Gestalt therapy will recall the basic tenet of empowerment through the here and now. In our work, we help men experience their here and now by noticing sensations inside as they are responding to their situation outside, by opening the heart and head to what's happening here now.

Leonard is a quiet, gentle fifty-five-year-old man married

to a woman as dynamic as Leonard is reserved. In fact Leonard's wife is the one who first encourages him to attend the Men's Room weekend. Upon arrival Leonard proceeds to spend most of his time on the sidelines, trying to figure out how this work applies to his own life, and specifically what might he be missing. He notices that there is something missing but, in reviewing his family life, his work situation, he can't find it. Near the end of the weekend it dawns on him and Leonard moves to the center to share his discovery.

"In my entire life," he declares, "I have never heard nor uttered the words, 'I love you,' either from or to my mother or father. Nor for that matter have I ever made real contact with either one of them, not ever. They were good parents, loving parents. They attended every event of significance for me, they fed and clothed me and they loved me, but I never heard it or received it in a hug. There was no real, no direct contact. And I . . . I tell them only what they want to hear. Everything else I leave out."

What Leonard goes on to describe is a "vast emptiness" that exists between him and his parents. "It is a distance that I'm talking about, um . . . and I believe I am this way myself. I'm this way with my wife, my kids. There is a distance I maintain in all my relationships. Right now I am seeing why my wife was adamant about me coming. I agreed to come, to be agreeable, because this is how I am. But until now I didn't have a clue as to how I might find the weekend useful.

"My mother and father are in their eighties. They may think I've lost my mind, but I intend to stop at their home on my way home, hug them, tell them I love them, that I want to hear them say it and that I need to say it finally. I want to show them what I've learned. I never thought I would ever consider anything like this. I feel like I've been holding my breath. Now I can breathe."

Leonard calls us later with a report. His parents were surprised but responded warmly to his openness. Next he asked his wife to sit with him and listen. In recalling the weekend he began to cry, and he told her then how much he loved her. He apologized for creating and keeping the distance and asked for her help in adding closeness, keeping aware, saying how he really feels and listening to her. When he is finished telling the story he laughs and adds, "My wife says I am a changed man."

Leonard is still a distant man. What he's doing is behaving differently. He's making contact, the only way to decrease the distance. Noticing it and then acting differently. Noticing is about two things: awareness and acceptance. First, you have to see it. "Whoops, there it is." In accepting it, you certify, "Yep, that's me, all right." Once you are present in the moment, you can focus on doing things a little differently and you can feel the results of your actions immediately. All things come back to us—connection or cut-off. Distance is a part of Leonard's character, but he can alter its effect on his relationships by being present, fully conscious of what is going on, and then making the effort to connect.

Avoiding eye contact is another sign of distance. It's as if we're saying, "Don't notice me and I won't notice you." Like the emperor with no clothes on. There is a nakedness, a kind of in-your-face impact to 100 precent presence, a laser-like attention that can be uncomfortable. As we move into presence, choosing to notice everything that is happening inside and outside of us, what we begin to see, hear, taste, take in with all our senses, may not always be pleasant, but it is powerful.

Have you noticed, for example, when you are working on a project, making a gargantuan effort but not much progress? One of the elements that makes or breaks the flow in work as well as in relationships is the degree of presence we bring to them. If we listen and speak with presence, those around us have a greater sense of satisfaction and completion about the contact. Listening with full presence, especially, requires a clear head and an open heart. The question now arises, how do we achieve this clarity and openness?

Shifting into Balance

The invocation to change is enough to make many men break out in hives. In The Men's Room we do not urge men to change because it often implies giving something up. Even if it were possible this is not our goal. Instead we talk about shifts, and we note that making a shift in behavior is easier with the support and encouragement of others who are also motivated to make shifts in their own lives.

Shifting does not mean substituting one kind of behavior for another. The object is to view all behavior as if it were on a continuum. For example, some of us act out of a strong logical orientation, relying on our heads to guide our behavior. Others may act primarily out of emotion, depending more on feelings or guidance from the heart. Neither of these orientations (head or heart) is right or wrong. We need both. The issue is balance. Too much head, not enough heart can pull us off balance, and vice versa. Virtually all of our behavior can be viewed in this way. Here are some further examples:

Serious	—	Playful
Competitive	—	Cooperative
Demanding	—	Giving
Cautious	—	Risk Taking
Active	—	Reactive
Critical	—	Supportive
Fast	—	Slow
Head	—	Heart

Picturing these paired behaviors as opposite ends of a see-saw or teeter-totter that you're standing on is a way to visualize what we mean by balance. By maintaining an equal share on both sides you stay balanced and keep the teeter-totter in a horizontal position. If you move exclusively toward one end, however, you'll go down with that end while the other flies upward. To regain balance you'll have to add weight (move toward) the other end. It involves *addition,* not subtraction. And although the ends represent opposites, both kinds of behavior are essential to balanced living.

The Magic Three

When we find ourselves operating repeatedly on one end of a continuum, it is usually because this behavior worked for us earlier in our lives. For a time it got us what we needed. Central to our willingness to make a shift is to be able to recognize when we are stuck at one end of a behavioral continuum. The best way to find out is from those closest to us. Here's a rule of thumb we use. If you hear something about yourself, a criticism perhaps, from just one person . . . in all likelihood this is idiosyncratic. It's just that person. If you hear the same or a similar thing about yourself from two people, give the issue some consideration. If you get the same feedback from three people, then know that it's real. This is a shift you need to make. Think of the positive opposite, the behavior you may need to add to bring yourself into balance.

Critical Shifts

There are some common shifts for men to make. One concerns moving from a critical stance to one that is approving. Think of a continuum with highly critical on one end and entirely approving or supportive at the opposite end. Many of us who are regularly critical of the people with whom we are in relationship—our wives, our children, our co-workers —were exposed as children to a highly critical parent or authority figure. In an attempt to be "good" we brought the critical parent inside of ourselves—making this "voice" a permanent part of us. In this way the nay-sayer is always on hand to remind us what not to do. In order also to think well of ourselves, we push or project the negative message outward onto others, just like our parents did to us. What comes around goes around.

Boyish and handsome, Kirk looks as if he might slip deftly into a Calvin Klein line-up. A brooding presence and dark eyes indicate a hollow coupling of youth and innocence in this young man. By late Saturday morning he is comfortable with the concepts of shifts and sensations. Anxiously he describes the sensation as one of "pressure building inside, nothing I can stop and so it feels like I'm going to shatter, you know, boom! like that." And this propels him into the center, the first of eighteen men to step forward this weekend.

If there is one scene from childhood, there are a thousand essentially the same. Arriving home late his father storms through the house demanding and sputtering: "Where's the newspaper? Who left the bike on the porch? The lawn is burning up. This whole place is a fucking wreck. Where is that good-for-nothing Kirk!"

When he locates the boy he smacks him up side the head and Kirk goes reeling. The father persists, kicking him, snarling obscenities, berating the boy until he quits out of exhaustion or wants to eat or have another drink.

Many times Kirk runs away to a neighbor's house or hides until his father has passed out, but the beating is worse if he puts it off. Kirk's mother tries to get between them, but this only nets her the first beating. She stops trying and simply stands by, whimpering, "Please don't." At age seven, eight, nine years old, these are the days and nights of life. Kirk remembers little else. He is not sure of what shift to make. He wants to root out the past, get rid of it so that he can get on with his life.

We suggest that Kirk select someone in the group who can

role-play the father, and also someone to represent his eight-year-old self. Kirk doesn't hesitate to pick out Mike, the tallest and largest man present to be his father. For his eight-year-old-self he picks Jonathan who is thin and intense.

Mike takes to the center at once and with startling gusto transforms himself into 250 pounds of scowling nastiness. With clenched teeth he begins to berate and threaten the eight-year-old Kirk, played by Jonathan, who is sitting cross-legged on the floor. Kirk stands behind Jonathan, leaning over him so the father can't get to the little boy. The father is on a rampage, yelling, "What're you doin'? Why isn't the garbage emptied? This room is a pigsty! One of these days I'm gonna break your neck."

Kirk returns the fire. "Shut up, don't talk to this kid that way, get the hell out of here. Get out of my face. I hate you."

Little Kirk, the child, is by now curled up in a ball against Kirk's legs. Kirk is guarding the child's face and head with one hand while shaking his fist at the father, "Get outta here, you bastard! You drunken slob. You don't belong here!"

The more Kirk yells at the father, the closer and more menacing the father gets. "I'm gonna tear you apart you little piece of crap, I'll teach you some respect if I have to kill you."

The child has buried his face, turned away and is clinging to Kirk's legs. To reassure him, Kirk bends down and puts both arms around him while shouting up to the father, "I'm not letting you near him, you're not going to touch him, you make me sick."

The father moves closer, "Why you punk, you . . . I'm . . ." And the child interrupts now with a wail. Kirk takes the child in his arms saying, "Don't worry, I won't let him hurt you. He can't touch you with me here."

As Kirk attends to the child the father quiets down and watches. When Kirk yells at the father again, the father goes after the child, snarling and yelling at the top of his lungs and Kirk screams back at him in a full rage.

The volume of anger in the room is ear-splitting. The child goes nuts, he's lost in fear, screaming "No, No! Stop! Don't let him hurt me!"

Kirk comes back to the child. "It's okay, it's okay," he reassures him. "I'm here. He can't hurt you now, I'm with you. We won't pay attention to him. Listen to me, I'll take care of you." Kirk gets down on the floor and wraps himself around the child, rocking and soothing him.

When the action centers on Kirk and the child, the father grows still as if released from cue. Kirk tells the child (his own inner child), "I promise I'll take care of you. I'll always be here for you. He's scary but he can't hurt you now." The father sits down, his energy depleted as Kirk gives himself over to the child, reassuring him, rocking and humming to him. Tears of relief streak their faces as they are delivered out of anger into the moment.

Of the men circling it is impossible to distinguish tears from sweat. Awed and drained they stand to honor the work. It is fairly amazing how close the drama comes to re-enactment. Anger hasn't moved anything, doesn't change anyone. No matter how much rage he vents, Kirk cannot get his father to withdraw. He could not as a child and he cannot now. He cannot kill off the father. He can, however, take care of the eight-year-old inside of him who is still experiencing the fear, the injury. When Kirk turns his full attention to tending to the child, the father fades. If we passed out scripts for this piece we could not come closer to the truth. For Kirk, life has been a constant fight of self-depreciation and avoidance. Internalize father or run from him. Now, shifting from critical to supportive, from angrily demanding to giving, he opens a new door.

Every Man

We say in The Men's Room that every man's piece (issue) is everyman's piece. Some says it's also everyman's peace. In

Kirk's work we connect with the father or authority who hurt us, who brings up the rage—for whatever reason—because he was hard on us or too soft, present or absent, fool or tyrant, whoever he is to our eight-year-old selves, or our four-, five-, or fifteen-year-old selves, however old we were at point of impact. Like Kirk we learn he cannot be driven off. The only way to get what we want is to tend to our own child.

There is more. Reaching beyond anger to care for his own injury opens Kirk up to caring for other people's injuries. Yet there is an obstacle. As Kirk puts it, "I would love to marry but I am afraid. It never seems to work out. Women I thought were right, end up irritating me. I get angry and break off. It's not so easy. The closer I get the more difficult they seem and the harder I am on them—not physically, but in how I treat them."

The major shift for Kirk is to move from being a bully to being a brother. This will be a shift he needs to make in every relationship—from critical to supportive, exacting to giving. The key to working this shift is the realization and acceptance of how he has presented himself all these years. "I am Sidney's son. I have an abuser in me. It comes from being abused."

We see the darkness and we accept it. The instinct is (as it was) to flee or fight—to deny it or get rid of it. But there is no psycho-surgical maneuver to make. It's not about subtraction. In self-recognition, bringing him or her into conscious consideration, we have the option of managing the abuser within. At the same time we begin consciously to give approval, to provide support to ourselves and others.

On the opposite side of this continuum are those who are too approving of others. The dynamic is similar. In this case we give approval because we can only bear to receive approval, feeling much too vulnerable to accept even the slightest criticism. It is as if we are permanently set on the side of support, of self and other. The shift here is to actually become more critical, to add a degree of critical and evaluative behavior reminding ourselves that we can expect to be criticized on occasion. The key is to be willing to call things authentically as we see them, to stop fudging and equivocating. We aren't protecting anyone (another or ourselves) by holding back our authentic feelings. The discovery in this shift is to see that criticism does not destroy us or anyone else. Again, the goal is to reach the point of balance along the continuum and then to maintain it by remaining aware, conscious in the moment, and then making adjustments as we discover the need.

Blocks to Balance

So far we have introduced the basic concepts of noticing, presence, body awareness, shifts, and balance and how these concepts affect our relationships. Now we'd like you to take a look at what stops you from acting in your own behalf. What blocks or interferes with your ability to make a shift once you decide on it?

Blocks come to us as fear—fear of loss of affection, fear of abandonment or failure, or even fear of success. Some of us fear disappearing or dying. We may have a deep conviction that we are not worthy, or that if we move in any direction the situation will get worse. We might see nothing but loneliness ahead or fear that we can't handle the consequences of an action. A block can show itself in anger, be tied to a dependency, or used to camouflage weakness.

Fundamentally our blocks represent tactics we once adopted instinctively under pressure to protect ourselves. They may have begun as a child's promise to him or her self that has carried a magical and prohibitive potency into adulthood. Unconscious and automatic, blocks remain in play regardless of their usefulness. When life circumstances change and require a different response, these strategies re-emerge as blocks that prevent us from taking care of ourselves in the present. They show up first in the body, often as pain or tightness—signaling the warfare within. Remember that sensation precedes emotion and therefore can guide us to the origin of a block whether it be of grief, fear, or a strategy to safeguard the ego.

Any thing or any emotion that blocks us from our full repertoire of feelings and responses reduces our presence, our potency, our power. What follows is one man's experience of pushing through his early childhood promise never to let his anger be seen.

Malcolm is thirty-eight years old. He looks open and dependable. There is a generosity about him—inside and out—reflected in his ample 5' 11" frame. Not fat, but large and soft. No visible muscle warns of any undisclosed anger or resistance. He is relaxed and open. His sandy brown hair and watery blue eyes convey the same fluid soulfulness he brings to every interaction. Here is a man with no competitive edge, who need not excel publicly, nor even strut on occasion. Nonetheless this seemingly satisfied soul enters the circle of men clearly troubled.

He tells of one Sunday afternoon when he suggests to his wife, Susan, that they take their three-year-old daughter Rachel with them for an early dinner out. Here they are in the restaurant, a family place where children are welcome. In marches a troop of six bikers dressed head to foot in black leather laced with silver studs. Initially the men walk right by Malcolm's family en route to an empty table. Suddenly the leader does a U-turn and comes back to get a closer look at three-year-old Rachel.

This is not an unusual occurrence because, as Malcolm explains to us, Rachel is stunning. She has an aura about her, "a wonderful spiritual presence," he calls it, to which many are drawn.

When all six bikers form a human wall around the edge of their booth, however, Malcolm is alarmed. They appear large, sweaty, and rough as they jostle each other for position and joke amongst themselves about "the cutest little doll in the world." Rachel is wide-eyed but unperturbed. Malcolm, on the other hand, sees danger drooling over her. And what he feels in the face of it is blind helplessness.

He is frozen with fear. Immobilized, he sees a gruesome sextet pat Rachel's hair, finger the ruffles on her dress, and gobble at her like a flock of wild turkeys. Malcolm moves his lips but no sound comes. He can only stare blankly straight ahead. In agony he turns to Susan for help. In this same instant Susan rises to her feet and in a quiet, I-mean-business voice she asks the bikers to please leave so the family can have dinner. Without pausing, all six men pat Rachel good-bye and amble off chortling to each other. From start to finish the episode lasts maybe three minutes tops. No harm done.

But Malcolm will never be the same. The realization that he is helpless to intervene when his family is in danger, as he sees it, is devastating. Susan makes light of it, but Malcolm sinks in an ocean of shame. Now he comes forward eager for dry land one way or the other. He needs no clues where to start or what he wants.

In his view it is clear-cut. His father was a tyrant, and early on Malcolm vowed to be opposite. His obvious success is testimony to the depth of a child's resolution. He is not unhappy with the result. The question he raises now is, Does he have any capacity to engage the enemy when necessary? Does he have that other stuff in him? The ability to express anger directly, to mobilize it as an effective source of strength? Or is this lost to him?

Malcolm is asked to describe his father's anger and his father's power. He calls it "a storm—lightning fast, white hot, electrical and dangerous." And Malcolm's own anger, how would that look and where might it rest in his body? "I don't know," he answers. "It's bluish. Not so quick. Takes time to find. It isn't in my body at all. It's in my head."

"Is your head attached?" a voice ventures out from the circle of men around him. Malcolm turns to look at the inquisitor and smiles broadly in response.

We set the scene as follows. Malcolm chooses a man to play his father. Malcolm will go up against the raging father to discover what he's made of. Then we assign one man to restrain each of Malcolm's arms, one man for each leg, and a fifth to grab hold of his belt and hold him back from behind. In this way Malcolm is contained. His challenge is to go after the raging intimidator. He's not only going after the father, he's going to have to drag five men with him.

Here is the soft male who feels thoroughly vulnerable physically, who is looking for the hardness, the muscles that live in his body which he's rejected out of hand because they mean *father* to him, they mean *violence,* they mean *horror.* Most important, there was a time when to be absolutely still, immobile, head separate from body muscle was the best strategy. As a child, Malcolm didn't stand a chance against his father. He carries his anger in his head, he says, as if it didn't exist (it's only in his head). Fear of physical threat engages the block between head and body. For Malcolm to work this shift from passive to assertive he needs to break the block and reconnect head to body, allowing the anger to circulate, mobilize, fuel the heart's desire and find effective outlet.

On the first round with the father taunting him, Malcolm gets going but goes nowhere. He's into it with a little bit of his head, a bit of arm, some leg, some spit, a little sweat, but the five men hold him squarely in place. He's diffused. The energy is off in all directions but forward. We stop the action. He has to learn to be still, yet feel the energy.

Close your eyes, we instruct. Breathe. Find the anger in your head. Start at the nose, take a deep breath inward, let the air open you up all the way down to the center of your being. Let the anger in your head follow the flow of air deep into your body. Breathe out slowly through your mouth. Take in another deep breath, let it wrap around all of the blue stuff in your head and bring it on down through your chest, all the way down to the center of your being. Now, inside your gut, feel the new energy you have. It's going to start growing. Let it grow, feel it build.

We see him breathing, beginning to build. His head straightens up and we tell him to focus his eyes on the object of his rage. He sees his father who starts taunting him again. Malcolm lunges forward! He struggles. It's more formed now . . . but it's not there yet. He struggles harder. His breath is growing short. He's exhausting himself.

Bob stops the action and lets him know he has one more chance to find the energy. At this point he hasn't moved forward but an inch or two. He is opened up. You can see the energy building inside but he's hesitating to release it. We review the instructions. Start over with the breathing, bringing everything down to the center of his being. He's got to keep still, until he's really feeling it, letting it build, feeling it rise to his chest, pushing it into his legs and arms, filling him and rising up, all the way back up into the head. "Open your eyes," we tell him. "Focus, make that connection, and *use* that connection to mobilize yourself."

The father is three or four feet away and taunts: "C'mon, you sissy! C'mon c'mon c'mon. You haven't got it, this is bullshit. You're never going to get to me, you pussy." And with that, Malcolm *lunges*. He's unified. All five guys go with him, he's dragging them, he's moving forward. The entire room starts cheering: "Go! Go! Go! Go! Get 'em! Get the fucker! Go Go Go Go!" They're applauding and they're moving in on him.

Every man is with him. Each one is thinking, "You gotta make it, you gotta get there. You gotta get him!" They're in there with the neighborhood bully or the brother who used to go after them or whoever it is who intimidated them. We're all right there, yelling at the top of our lungs and Malcolm is dragging five men across the room. He's not stopping. His teeth are bared. He's spitting, sweat is flaring off of him, snot pouring down his face. His shirt is soaked and he's still moving forward. The sound is indescribable.

In our delirium we nearly forget . . . this is not about getting the father. It's about Malcolm finding his force. He's found his force. He's connected with the anger, his own anger, his rage, different from his father's rage. He's found it. We stop the action and we ask him, "Can you feel it?"

He growls back, "Yes, I feel it."

Now we ask him, "Where is it?"

First Malcolm holds up both hands, fingers spread, palms flat outward, as if he were about to stop an oncoming locomotive. He shouts: "It's in my hands. And it's in my eyes! In my eyes!" he repeats.

"Now what will you do when the men come to your table?" we ask. "I will raise my hand up, I will make eye contact, and I will say, Stop!" It's in the eyes now. We can all see it. His gaze is like steel. The softness is gone from the eyes. The muscles in his face move, his jaw is set. At this moment we stop and ask Malcolm to go around the room and tell every man that he will stop them when necessary, and he will let them enter when he wants. Twenty-two times he makes the approach, declaring to each: "I will stop you. Or I will let you in if I choose."

He's got it. It's under his control, not his father's. The connection is made between body and head. It is not in the use of physical force. For Malcolm it is in finding the power in his eyes, the focus, the connection, taking back the ability to see, to face the unfaceable, to see it, to move on it. Gone is the "blind helplessness" and relentless repetition of the terror from childhood trauma. In recognizing and moving through the block, adding the firmness and assertiveness, Malcolm has moved decisively toward a healthy balance between passive and assertive.

One More Round

There is another piece here. Malcolm has developed and utilized his softness to guard against being anything like the father. His belief on this level is that muscle = violence. Engaging his own muscle may also mean facing his own violence, perhaps even his own abusiveness. He is his father's son. What goes around comes around. In this regard his discovery that the muscles he feels in his body can be used through the eyes is significant. Notice that Malcolm's anger starts out in his head and even after the block is removed remains there (albeit mobilized and expressed through the eyes). Our unconscious mind instructs us, as if it knows precisely, uncannily, what to keep and what to let go.

As with all the work in The Men's Room, the issues raised by Malcolm's work present questions for all of us to answer. Can I be strong and powerful without being violent? Can I use my muscle to good effect? How can men be strong and potent and not be violent? How do we manage the violence within?

In Relationship

Born into a time and place where relationships are under siege and malnourished from a lack of family and community support, we have a need to re-create an environment in which they can thrive. Perhaps the most vital ingredient here is personal accountability. Embracing the notion of "What I am I cause to be," we acknowledge the effect of our actions and honor our commitment to take responsibility for creating our own future. What goes around comes around. We are also affected by the actions of others. There is a mutual causality at work. But if our goal is to build healthy relationships the first question to ask is, What am I bringing to an interaction that is creating this result?

Taking full responsibility is a two-edged sword. It puts us at risk by putting us out there in front, stating who we are, what we feel, what we believe, and what we're willing to do. It means we have to come clean about what is difficult, what we don't like, or what makes us uncomfortable. It also gives us the fullest, most expansive quality of life imaginable in what comes back to us.

In this chapter we have discussed developing awareness, noticing what it is we think and feel, what our sensations are, becoming present in the here and now of relationships, developing balance in our lives, and discovering the blocks to shifts we want to make. When this process of self-examination is begun we are prepared to enter into and maintain much better, long-lasting, intimate relationships with the people in our lives. Before moving to the next chapter, you might stop, get quiet, and consider in some depth a shift you would like to make in your own life. Write it down and keep it somewhere visible, where you are reminded from time to time that it is a possibility and an opportunity for you.

THREE

Intimacy and Health

If you always do what you've always done,
you'll always get what you've always gotten.
—Anonymous

■ **Recently** the two of us gave a talk on gender sensitivity to about 150 employee assistance program professionals. In our presentation we focused on men in relationship with each other, their spouses, partners, children, parents, friends, and colleagues. Our work over the past ten years has taught us over and again that good health for men depends upon our ability to enter into and maintain ongoing, intimate relationships with other people. In this chapter the issue is communication: how the ways we communicate open us to intimacy or keep us closed off from it.

First we need to look at how our priorities influence the way we communicate.

Man as Money Machine

Once a young man enters the working world, there is intense pressure for him to focus exclusively on earning a living and providing or preparing to provide for a family. He must learn to conform outwardly and inwardly to the desired persona as conveyed by his superiors, learn to stifle those parts of himself and his actions that are not deemed appropriate. At work he is also in direct competition with his peers to win approval and advance through the system. Consequently many men suffer from chronic and painful isolation—systematically removing themselves from supportive association with each other outside the "acceptable" realms of business, politics, and sports. Often men endure a parallel isolation at home from meaningful intimate relationships with their families because their top priority (and measure of self-worth) is to survive and move forward at work.

It is falsely assumed that men want it this way. Also false is the assumption that this choice is in accordance with men's nature. For years some women have expressed anger over men's supposed predisposition to remain at a distance emotionally. In reality this is but one group's definition of man's nature and its intention for him to behave according to its rules and preferences. As one colleague puts it, "The decision was made by a handful of powerful industrialists followed by a hundred years of breaking men's collective spirit."

While nobody sat down and made a plan as such, one dominant mode of human interaction today, especially in the work place, was established on the heels of the industrial revolution. As the machine became the major energy source for productive life and collective survival, much of our lives were tailored to match and support it. Although we've moved along into the Information Age, the underpinning of industrial culture remains with its exclusive emphasis on logical, mechanistic, impersonal interaction. In this paradigm, men (and now women) become what the job requires. (As the new money making machines, women—to the extent they are pressured to conform to an outdated and rigid character ethic at work—suffer similarly.) Significantly, what the job requires are interchangeable parts at every level, where the goal is never defined in human terms, always in economic terms, and fulfillment is defined by the Gross National Product.

An interchangeable part does not have an emotional history—joys or sorrows, wounds, scars, or unique personality. Certainly it has no biochemical or genetic predisposition, no heritage, nor does it know a spiritual life. It does not have sick or elderly parents or children who suffer from want of attention. It may have a work history, an on-the-job or out-of-home past, embellished by certain kinds of education. All else is not only irrelevant, it gets in the way. So the adage goes, "Leave your troubles (and all things experienced on the human and personal level) on the doorstep."

The emotional distance of men is in no small part a result of these economic priorities. They influence how, when, and if we communicate, and they continue to shape and mis-shape our assumptions about who men are and what they want.

When given the opportunity and the means to discover their own capacity for another way of being in the world, our collective experience with men tells us they invariably say Yes. But without the support and encouragement of other men and women, without a society that beckons men forth instead of pushing them back, without the realization that we do indeed have the capacity to change, men will repeat the past and remain in isolation where, as Lillian Rubin in *Intimate Strangers* points out, they become "friends of the road instead of friends of the heart."

When an arena is provided for men to let down the barriers they open like a river undammed. Feelings take a natural course rather than being subverted and denied only to erupt in ill health, addiction, violence, or in any one of numerous unwarranted and unhealthy places. It is natural for all human beings to make their true selves known, to seek active, close, involved, contact with other people. When men are able to pull together the different aspects of their lives through authentic expression in close relationship with others, they thrive.

The Man in Control Myth

During our presentation to this professional gathering we came to focus on the degree to which men and women stereotype and pigeonhole each other. One woman spoke passionately of the depression women suffer as a result of having to stifle their anger (as those with less power often must do). Stifling anger, she presumed, is the domain of women. But many men are nothing short of phobic about the expression of anger—their own or anyone else's. Most likely some women are also depressed due to loss or shame or an inability to express a range of feelings or perhaps because they may feel incapable of entering into meaningful intimate relationships—the same as it is for many men.

Though the issue is publicly avoided, our experience as corporate consultants and that of our colleagues suggests that many women who have joined the out-of-home work force, whether from desire, necessity, or both have acquired behaviors and responses similar to the corporate men who have gone before them. These include becoming more competitive, demanding, problem solving, cold, aloof, and eager to turn on the TV and turn off the day. Other women are returning to the unpaid home force, if they can afford it, because they have seen how the world of work outside slowly removes affect, color, and vitality from their lives. What was once attractive and forbidden is looking progressively unappealing. Thus while men are asking, "Isn't there more to life than making money?" women are raising the question: "How do we work the out-of-home territory and not lose the expressive, nurturing parts of ourselves that are part of female heritage—qualities without which a society cannot remain civilized?" Behavior once confined to one gender role or another is dissolving into the realm of merely human. With this change in perspective, hopefully we can move beyond some of the destructive elements in the polarization of the sexes.

Leaving the Road Well Traveled

Watching children play we see how naturally authentic and intimate we once were. How easily we once cried out our desires and pain, hopes and needs, fears and joys. By the time we reach adulthood we know that what comes naturally is not necessarily easy. Indeed, masking feelings, stifling expression, withholding vital information, enduring pain in silence, delaying pleasure, removing ourselves from ourselves in the moment is in large part the mark and measure of maturity in our society. It is to one extent or another for all adults a requirement.

When we get ready to undo our armor, feel our feelings, tell the truth, reach out to touch or be touched, ask for help—to make a shift in our lives—at first we hardly know where to begin. Mountains were moved and years spent making the road well traveled. As we peer into the surrounding wood our hearts skip a beat, for the path appears to have vanished. Warily we step into this dark forest. It helps now to remember that we have been here before. Going again we gather in pairs and groups like children on a nighttime treasure hunt.

In The Men's Room, we begin to *be* again, to find the moment lost or stillborn. And we start here with what's happening to us now. One man, upon being asked, "What do they do in The Men's Room?" answered:

*Aware of the dark, following dimly lit clues sketched upside
down in the margins of days long gone, we let ourselves be
guided by ancestors thumping at the door of our waking,
singing and laughing and longing to be recognized. We hold
onto each other jostling along, careful not to slip off the
edge. Emerging path's imaginary ledge. Shouting we encourage the slowest among us, we clap and pick up the pace stepping up to enormous shapes and sounds, to beasts unknown
who growl and moan and disappear in a whisper as we glide
by. A longish, bumpety outline snaking through the bush
breakneck now until the first of us cracks through, bursts out
into amazing space, a glorious opening inside remembered
place by us now and each in turn in time will tumble himself into the light.*

A Little Respect

For as long as Fred can remember, he wants his father to
show him respect, to acknowledge his abilities and efforts.
Fred's father founded and heads up a substantial corporation.
At age forty-three with fifteen years experience, Fred feels capable of directing the organization. Yet at every opportunity
his father points out how Fred is lacking in a number of
essential qualities.

"I beg him to give me responsibility for new projects,"
Fred tells us. "The business is growing. Marketing needs over-
haul. Last week he brings in someone from outside for the
job, ignoring all the times I pleaded for the go-ahead. He
walks into my office cold and says, 'Son, this is Ralph Steigler.
He's our man. He's gonna do it for us. Give him everything
he needs.'"

One of the men from the circle of men surrounding Fred
interrupts him. "Fred," he says, "the writing's on the wall.
Time for you to move on. What's the competition doing?"

Fred answers, "No way. You sound like my wife. This is
where I belong. I know the operation better than he does

now—details he doesn't mess with. I can't leave. It's my dream, and my nightmare. My father and I might not get on that well. I mean . . . I respect him. He's taught me everything. But it's killing me. It's driving my wife nuts. But no, I can't leave. Besides, it would kill my mother. She counts on me. See, my father is . . . he's real smart. He knows more about more things than anybody I know. But he gets carried away. Makes decisions too fast. Most of them are good. But a lot of our top people don't care much for him. They live with him, but if I left, I don't know . . . Then we would have problems with the competition. When I try to explain it to him, he says, 'Who? You're nuts. You don't know people. That's another one of your problems, kid. Let them leave! Now, quit whining and get outta here, I've got a company to run.' If he would just give me credit. I can't tell you what I do for the guy and what I get for it. Last week I showed Ralph how to save us five hundred grand. Ralph is okay. He told Dad flat out, 'Fred put me onto this.' And you know what my Dad said? 'Good job Ralph. This is why we hired you.'"

The men look on in silence. We set up a role play for the work. Fred picks Rick, the man who suggested he quit, to be his father. We take Rick aside first and instruct him to play the father to the hilt. Exaggerate. We ask Fred to tell his father what he wants from him, everything he wants from him. Don't hold back. We're all with you. Get what you need from him this time. (*Rick starts the action.*)

Father: Okay, son, I'm busy this morning, make it short, will you?

Fred: Well, Dad, don't worry, this won't take long. It's just that . . . um, well, what I really want to do is talk . . . and, um, maybe get some things clear here between us.

Father: Get to the point.

Fred: Well, as you know, I'm counting on taking over for you some day and I thought, well, we might talk about when that could be? A timeline. And then some related things that need to be done.

Father: You're wasting my time. Get to the point.

Fred: Well, when do you see me taking over? Two years, five years? Ten?

Father: When I'm dead. That's when. Son, please. This discussion is stupid. Let's just get back to work. Close the door on your way out, I've got some calls to make.

Fred: No, we've gone on like this for too long. I need some answers now. We have planning to do. There are decisions . . .

Father: (*interrupts*) Enough! This is a perfect example of why you're not ready. In the first place you're too soft. Yeah, you're good at this and that. Yeah, you did okay with this project and that one. But you always want a medal for just doing your job. I don't give out medals and I don't give out companies. You've been here what, how many years and you're wet. Wet and green. You're a nice boy. Everybody likes you. Hooray. You're too soft. You've always been too soft. And this is it . . . you come sniveling in here like your mother when she wants a new coat. That's another thing. I don't like saying this, but you're a bit of a . . .

Fred is waving one finger sideways as if to stop his father's words from coming. He tries several times to get a word in edgewise . . . then he waits . . . then he tries again but the father ignores him and continues to berate him, demanding to know why he would ever give in to such a wimp. Fred puts his hands over his ears and starts saying, No, no, no. But Rick as the father keeps right on going, raising his volume. Fred's hands are shut into fists at his sides. The low growling noise we hear starts as he raises both fists up over his head. His color has gone from white to red.

The men in the circle around him are moving in. Fred is too close to Rick and Rick is still hammering away verbally, seemingly oblivious to the change in Fred's demeanor. For a split second everyone is thinking the same thing and they are moving in to stop it. Fred's growl rises to a roar as he brings both fists down. Across the circle six men crouch like quarterbacks poised for the hike. The fists come down in slow motion before they slam into Fred's own thighs and he roars: "Shut the fuck up! This is my company too! I've built it up just like you! If you won't give me what is mine I'll take it from you lock stock and barrel, you goddamned fool!"

In the beginning, and this is true for all of us when we get stuck, Fred cannot see his own contribution to the never ending battle. The exaggerated role play in a removed and safe environment allows the frustration level to build to the breaking point in seconds. The explosion gives vent to a rage that this "good boy," this "mama's best boy" never before dared express. Purged of its grip, he is able to move through it. The first rush of joy comes from experiencing his own power, taking charge. Fred's past failure is not due so much to his father's lack of faith as his own, the nay-saying father within. The good little boy who "begs and pleads" keeps getting kicked out of the ring. On the other side of his rage, Fred discovers a respect for this other son within him who knows he has the backbone to lead. Over the course of the weekend, he also uncovers a fatherly tenderness toward the polite little guy in him who isn't up to the task. So Fred learns he has the capacity to go forth—with this one or that one (politely or not so). It is different because he sees himself differently. This is where the potential for a new outcome rests. Often curiosity follows new behaviors. This yields the potential for conversation that deepens relationship.

When he returns home, Fred asserts himself boldly in those areas of the business where he feels most competent. He stops going into his father to report each success, for he understands now that it isn't his father he needs to convince. Then he moves into new areas, neither asking permission nor showing up with an apology when things don't go so well.

Not four months pass before Fred's father starts coming around to visit him, at first to request lots of information. He begins on some of these occasions to compliment Fred on some of his efforts and now he also asks for his son's advice directly. The relationship does not change overnight, but it is headed in a new direction.

The best episode for Fred is when his father shows up to thank him for handling a difficult, politically charged situation in a senior staff meeting, saying, "You know, Fred, I've got to admit I'm just not any good at that kind of thing. You handled it perfectly." It was the first time Fred could remember his father admitting to a personal weakness and also the first time he acknowledged the value of Fred's style, very different from his own.

I Want to Be Loved by You

Dennis is quiet, respectful, and cool. He keeps his distance from the other men in attendance. When he finally speaks, he describes a slow grinding loneliness that is eating his marriage from the inside out. He's a businessman; she's an artist. He leaves early every morning. She sleeps late, runs the household, and then remains in her studio until late every night.

"We used to go out, do weekends with friends, go skiing," he says. "Now she's too busy. We have dinner together—unless she's too busy—and that's about it. When I mention my work or things happening to friends, she fades out like I'm only one channel on her set and she's decided to click over to something better. I can't touch her anymore, not really. She ices over as if she hates it, me. We don't fight, don't disagree hardly. It's horrible."

Dennis is depressed and by the time he finishes his story everyone is down. We ask Dennis if he's willing to play his wife Janie's part in a role play session, to show us how she behaves when he approaches her. Burt volunteers to be Dennis in the scene. Since Burt is a natural actor, the action in the heart heats up instantly as he bangs on the imaginary door, yelling:

Burt: Janie for God's sake open the goddamned door! (*Dennis starts to laugh but jumps toward the door and flings it open dramatically to match Burt's melodrama.*)

Burt: (*Without hesitating, scoops Dennis/Janie into his arms, swings him around, lets him go mid-air and crash to the floor while Burt continues striding across the floor shouting:*) What's for dinner honey, I'm starved!

Dennis: (*Still theoretically playing his wife Janie, breaks character and starts to laugh again, so hard he can barely get to his feet.*) Nut'n Honey! (*He shouts back to Burt, then adds in high whiny voice*) I've been so busy in my studio today and besides that I'm not hungry!

Burt: Nuttin?! (*He whirls around to face Dennis and then adds*) Well, hell, let's have sex instead. Come here you gorgeous thang, you. I'm gonna eat you up! (*He threatens while he moves toward Dennis.*)

Dennis: (*who hasn't stopped laughing since the scene began, shrieks in a high voice*) No you're not! Don't you touch me! (*as he starts scooting sideways around the circle like a wrestler preparing for the onslaught of the Hun*)

Burt: (*Scooting after Dennis teasing*) Oh c'mon now, you cutie-wootie. You know I'm gonna get you. Don't even try to put me off. (*He rushes in and grabs Dennis' arm.*)

Dennis: (*Wrenching his arm free, yells angrily in a gruff voice*) Cut it out now!

Meanwhile the rest of the room is in an uproar, laughing and shouting out encouragement to Burt's characterization of Dennis, "Go get her, Dennis!" somebody shouts. And another man squeaks in a high voice, "C'mon little Janie, be a good sport! He only wants to give you a little lovin'. He's your man!"

With Burt's clowning in the role of Dennis, the mood has swung from morose to a shrill exuberance. Everyone is caught up in blowing off the initial tension and sadness in this frenzied, aggressive caricature. It is not the role play we anticipated. No one is more delighted than Dennis. For a few minutes he lets go and joins the play. When he drops out of character and tells Burt to "Cut it out," we stop the action and ask Dennis what's going on, where is he now? And he responds:

Dennis: I don't know, I feel like this is ridiculous. My wife is really sweet and . . . this isn't fair. So, what's the point?

[Bob/Buddy]: What's not fair?

Dennis: It's just not right. I mean we're not anything like this. It's a whole different thing.

[Bob/Buddy]: What's the difference? Tell us about the differences.

Dennis: (*Stammers for a bit, then declares*) Janie is very special. She's quiet and serious about her work . . . . I mean, I don't do stuff like this.

[Bob/Buddy]: Do you take her in your arms?

Dennis: Well, I try.

[Bob/Buddy]: How do you try?

Dennis: Well, not like him! (*He pokes a thumb in Burt's direction*) Not like that.

[Bob/Buddy]: Like what?

Dennis: Like rape! (*He snaps indignantly and then suddenly he laughs again recalling the hilarity*) I'll tell you what though? I wish it could be like this. I'm having a ball!

[Bob/Buddy]: Well, do you tease her? Do you play with her? Do you get down on your knees and beg her? Do you give what you want to get? Did you notice how Burt got you laughing? You liked it. It was surprising. Out of character, different . . .

Dennis: Yes.

We did the role play all over again in a more serious vein but not without laughter. In this safe environment, we take turns asking from each other what we want or think we want out there in the real world. In the exchange with each other we get clarity, focus, new information. In the safety of knowing every man here is working for the same thing, each man learns to seek out how this guy sees it, or that one, how we appear to others versus how we see ourselves. As Buddy and I risk ourselves, move into our own concerns and give to each other the warmth and support each of us needs, the men begin to get the idea. Risks are necessary, pain is everywhere, we are not alone. We not only can ask for help, it's the best thing to do. Asking is healing. It brings us closer. Giving what another asks moves us still further.

Dennis speaks of his fear of being ridiculed if he acts in a warm and sensitive manner. "Right," says Burt, "It's faggoty. That's what we used to say about the guys who were nice, never mind warm and sensitive." Now Burt continues. He's become thoroughly engaged in this:

"Even now the words bug me a little. Warm and sensitive. Like eeeeuuww, definitely faggoty. I know this is Junior High attitude and I should be over it now that my own kids are in Junior High, but it stays there to some extent even though I've been exposed to much better attitudes."

We ask Burt to explain . . . what does "much better" mean?

"Much better, in my case," he begins, "was my cousin Arthur from Brooklyn. After high school graduation I got a job working for my Uncle Milton and spent the summer living with Arthur and my aunt and uncle. Cousin Arthur, who at ten years old was totally normal and the neatest guy in the world, turns out at eighteen to be a real live out-of-the-closet-except-his-parents-don't-know homosexual. He meets me at the airport, races up, grabs my arm and pumps it, gives me a hug and says, 'Burt, guess what, I'm queer, and if you tell Mom and Dad you're dead!' No problem, I tell him, I'm cool.

"At that point Arthur had taken boxing lessons and some kind of martial art for five years already. He used to say 'Hurt makes more hurt. If they hurt me, they're gonna hurt more.'

"I learned more about people that summer than the next four years in college. Arthur dragged me, pardon the expression, through every gay bar in Manhattan. I spent the whole time moaning about it, but I loved every minute of it. It was like, oh my God, these guys are real. I couldn't wait to tell some of the guys back home what it's like. Not what you'd think. And you know what? I never did.

"You guys are the first to know because I figured anybody I told back then would think I was gay myself. But here's my point, while I met plenty of guys who are, you know, warm and sensitive, there's plenty more who aren't. You wanna see attitude, check out a gay bar. It's the same with women. Some of them are warm and sensitive. But count the ones who aren't! I've been watching Dennis go through this and I can see . . . yeah that's me . . . needing to be loved, but I don't want to ask for it and I sure as hell don't want to go warm and sensitive for it, until now. Now I see that somebody had better be warm and sensitive or it's not going to happen. I got it. Hey, I'm a sensitive guy."

When Dennis returned home he approached Janie very differently. He inquired after her day, how she was feeling about the things in her life. He started telling her how much he admired her accomplishments and how much he loved her. The effect took him by surprise. She greeted him with enthusiasm when he got home from work, and she started picking up some films they had wanted to see. She began to flirt and tease him a bit when they relaxed together. The level of mutual caring and intimacy grew in direct proportion to the degree that he took responsibility for the relationship.

Carry Me Home

James is going through a divorce. He has moved out, is in a new relationship, and the lawyers are negotiating. He sees his young son less and less, misses him terribly, worries about him. The son of divorced parents himself, James swore he'd never put a child of his through this. He wouldn't disappear. The lawyers are scrapping. His wife is furious with the proposed settlement.

James complains, "The whole thing is totally crazy. What does she think—everybody gets to eat but me? She's so hateful! I can't bear to think what she's telling my son. My stomach is in knots. I'm on the phone with my idiot lawyer half the day. I have to hold his fucking hand while the other one is screwing me and I'm giving them both my last dime? I'm not sleeping. I'm so behind at work I have to hide stuff, fake it. My girl friend doesn't want to hear about it. Last week she tells me if it doesn't stop she'll leave, she's sick of it. What does she think, I can call a halt to it? I'm going through this nightmare just to irritate her? I want to marry this woman and she's about to walk because she doesn't want to hear about my lousy divorce?"

We have James turn up the volume a bit and tell us more about how bad it is, every screwed-up thing, how he feels about it all. More! In a couple of minutes James works up a good lather. Then we stop the action and say, "Okay James, take a deep breath, put your heart into it, and repeat these words out loud: *Please love me. Don't abandon me. Please hold me. I need you to hold me and love me."*

James gets as far as "hold" in the third sentence, and he breaks. He just sits down and sobs. He let's it all go. All the *angst,* all the misery. He just gives it up when he is able to say what he wants, what he's feeling underneath all the stuff. Like so many of us, James wants someone to notice how badly he is hurting, he wants someone to read his mind. He wants permission to cry. We all need to be held and comforted. It has nothing to do with our age or size or sex or sexual preference.

And this is exactly what he finally tells his fiancée Donna, after role-playing the situation with one of the men in the group: "This is very painful for me to say, but have you got room for me to cry in your arms?" Donna is thrilled that James has come to her for honest consolation, which is what she wants to give him. Their relationship moves to a new level, because James has allowed himself to be vulnerable in this relationship.

Each of these men—Fred, Dennis, and James—is initially caught in a pattern of doing the same thing and feeling frustrated. First they have to articulate what they want to happen. Sometimes we feel ashamed of what we want. We can hide the truth of what we want from ourselves as well as others. Some men actually feel that wanting something at all is unmanly.

Think of yourself, of what you long for, of how wonderful it would be to speak it, to be heard, understood, accepted. You may not immediately receive what you want, you may get some now, perhaps all. More importantly, can you imagine the relief of speaking the truth, of becoming unbound? There is health in this sharing.

Fred knows he wants respect but must discover that self-respect comes first, and he has to find a way to get his long-standing, carefully stifled rage out of the way before he can begin to approach his father as an equal in the business. Dennis wants warmth, affection, and love but needs to see his own aloofness, coldness, and inability to express. He's got to give it before he's going to get it, to provide the kind of warmth that will open a way in for his wife.

James, on the other hand, is in the kind of pain that is unavoidable with crisis and loss. There is no way around it. Since he doesn't feel entitled to let go, to ask for help and the love that will get him through it, he has to keep up an endless complaining tirade just to relieve the emotional build up. The result is that he alienates everyone, especially the one person close enough to give him the support he needs. In this society we teach men to wreak havoc rather than cry. Everyone suffers for it.

The work here represents only a portion of the effort required, spent, and continued. Fred does not come to terms with his father all of a sudden. Fred will be coming to terms with his father for the rest of his life, even after his father is no longer living. Now that he's shifted his approach, however, he stands a much better chance of getting what he wants from the relationship.

The shifts these men make come out of a willingness to look into the mirror without blinking, to see themselves in a way they usually avoid or deny. In doing so, each man risks the ridicule and condemnation he has come to expect from peers if he tells his full story honestly. Our basic training conspires against this kind of opening up. In The Men's Room, success exists because the work takes place in a context of community, with other men intent on improving their own lives too.

In your community you can begin by finding one man, a chosen brother, to begin these conversations. Look for someone who smiles, is kind, generous, who possesses some openness. Begin slowly. Take steadily bigger steps. The healing will begin almost immediately.

Buddy and Emily

BUDDY ▼ I want to share a final example of the kind of shift we're talking about. My daughter Emily is a strong-willed, verbally adept high school freshman who has let me know that while she loves me very much and appreciates my love for her, she doesn't want to hear about it all the time. To her it's a nuisance when I express my feelings for her as frequently as I used to do. This was painful for me to hear and it wasn't easy for me to learn to approach her differently—which meant being patient, more receptive, and allowing her to initiate contact more often by expressing her own feelings first.

My father was a gentle, very loving, but quiet and re-served person. While we never experienced a lack of love from him, my brother and I learned it was inappropriate for us—first as boys and then as men—to express these feelings openly. The message was: Men can love but for God sakes be quiet about it. Don't be verbal, obvious, or too physical. Don't let it show. I probably always felt a cer-tain need to stifle myself in order to get it right. As an adult I resolved to assert my love actively with my own children.

In part my assertiveness prevented my daughter from setting the boundaries of her own comfort level, just as my father's reticence had done to me. I took control of an arena in which she also needs control. Also my actions tended to keep her from initiating contact. Where was the space for it? Furthermore, in seeing my disappointment she may well have felt that I needed something from her that she couldn't give. Children want to please their parents and sometimes it scares them when they can't, for whatever reason.

The most important shift for me to make with my daughter was to be more receptive in order to balance the assertiveness. Patience and acceptance were called upon to soften my tendency toward action and exertion. The block for me here, the reason it took time, work, and help to make the shift successfully involved: (1) my fear of losing out (on my daughter's love) unless I go for it in a big way first; (2) anger at not being able to express my feelings openly to my father and many others over the course of my life; and (3) my reluctance to perceive my daughter's resistance as a result of my own actions.

When I was able to see these blocks and move past them, I could be comfortable in my feelings without having to assert them each time and without feeling deprived. I could do so generously, do it for myself. In time Emily began to receive and return my affection more readily. She has gained a clear understanding that she has the right to assert her own desires whether they involve yes or no, if they please her father or not.

Another important polar continuum here has to do with quality and quantity. Too many I love you's sap the substance. Sometimes when we are preoccupied with expressing our love, we are indirectly asking for proof of the other person's feelings. The shift in this case would be to become more nurturing of ourselves instead of focusing on nurturing the other person. ▼

Love Numbers

We know that good communication is the foundation of a rewarding relationship. Achieving good communication between partners requires desire, commitment, and a willingness to work at it. Men may have the best intentions in this area, but they lack practice, tend to back away from emotional expression (theirs and their partners'), and often feel that it isn't safe to open up. Vulnerability is perceived as unmanly. This "opening up" and letting another human being in past the usual barriers we call *intimacy*. Some men are uncomfortable with the term because they're not sure what it means, how to do it, if they are capable of it—or even if they really want it. Intimacy has a feminine ring to it, a little frightening and at the same time exciting.

So with men it is important to define what we mean by intimacy and also provide some direction as to how to get there. First we need to de-mystify and de-feminize the term. Why, after all, should a need that all humans share for warmth and authentic contact be defined as feminine? In our culture this has been the case. The feminization of intimacy probably originates with our first intimate contact, usually with our mother, but it needn't stay there. Also, because homophobia runs deep in our society, we tend to associate intimacy in an all-male context with homosexuality. This is the source of some of our fear and hesitation. It may be helpful to point out that homosexuals don't find intimacy any easier to obtain and maintain in their relationships than heterosexuals. There is no connection, per se, between homosexuality and intimacy other than the human one.

The universal desire for intimacy grows out of an even more fundamental need on the part of every person to be *known*—to be recognized and accepted for exactly who they are, no more, no less. The operational definition we use for intimacy, whether at home or in the workplace, is: the ability to notice what is going on inside and outside of ourselves and the willingness to report it in a timely, authentic, and appropriate manner. This definition has no sexual or gender overtones. It is bare-boned, functional, practical, and accurate. When men hear this definition of intimacy they are comfortable with it. Furthermore, with this definition we can discuss intimacy in the work place.

In fact, a number of executives and CEOs attribute their success in part to a habit of (1) noticing when they feel uncomfortable about an interaction, (2) calling for a second meeting within 24–48 hours, and then (3) reporting this discomfort directly to the person or group involved so that a mutually satisfying conclusion or positive closure to an issue is reached. If corporations would encourage and reward intimacy of this kind at all levels, corporate life would gain a human element and a level of honest internal/external communication that is greatly needed.

Intimacy is not an all-or-none proposition. We experience it in different amounts, at different levels, for distinct lengths of time, and it serves diverse purposes from one occasion to the next. In The Men's Room we have developed a model to help us distinguish between different levels of intimacy. Since so many men love numbers, we have divided the levels of communication in relationship into four parts. We refer to these as the four levels of listening and speaking.

LEVEL I: *Small Talk*

Level I listening and speaking refers to the most superficial level of communication. Other labels we use for it are water cooler or cocktail conversation. There is not much contact between the communicators, no probing questions; it is a way to meet a social obligation, to speak without having to say much.

(Example of Level I)

Buddy: How you doing, Bob?

Bob: Oh, pretty good. It's a nice day. We're uh, you know, it feels pretty good to be doing some work out here in the park. All the greenery, smells wonderful, fresh and like Spring. Nice breeze, hmmm.

Buddy: Do you see the sailboat over there on Lake Michigan? Beautiful! You're still sailing, aren't you Bob?

Bob: Yeah, yeah. I am and uh, actually I've seen a couple of skate boarders go by, not skate boarders, the roller bladers, and thinking about when we're done here, I might go do some of that, get some exercise. How about you?

Buddy: Yeah, sounds good to me. It's exciting, you know, to be writing this book and already on the third chapter. What do you think?

Bob: Yeah.

LEVEL II: *Person to Person*

Level II listening and speaking is where most people have conversation. It is more focused than Level I, a little deeper in terms of real contact between people. It is often task and schedule oriented. When will you have the report finished? Can we have lunch on Friday? It is also fairly cognitive or intellectual and still superficial in terms of relational contact. Level II has more "I" statements than Level I, so that we're beginning to take more ownership and responsibility for the things that are spoken.

(Example of Level II)

Buddy: I feel like we're actually going to finish the book and it will have an impact. That feels good. Really good.

Bob: It feels good to me, too. I'm real excited about it. I'm curious though, what's the best part about it for you?

Buddy: Letting people know about the work. Ten years! And also what it might be like when more people know about it? There we'll be at a big time bookstore on a Saturday afternoon autographing books! So it's about ego and that kind of stuff, too.

Bob: Book signings, I love it! One thing I think about is long term. The legacy. Like my grandkids someday might say "That's my grand-dad. He did that!"

LEVEL III: *Interpersonal Contact*

Level III shows a deepening of contact between people, with more intense sharing. There is a closing of psychological distance, greater concentration of energy on the moment (greater presence), more probing underneath the surface of comments. Level III can seem one-sided in that one person may be engrossed in talk while the other is listening carefully. With Level III there is a shorter distance physically and psychologically between the speakers. There is demonstrable mutuality of interest and the feeling afterward is that significant contact has been made. A certain level of empathy pertains, hence the big role of the listener.

(Example of Level III)

Buddy: What gets me is the piece about my, um, you know, learning disability. The incongruity. How can a guy who can't read or write hit the bestseller list? Maybe Lucia's right, maybe it should be a play? I can act. And direct. And as for applause, well, as you know . . .

Bob: Never mind the applause, I want to know about your learning disability, what it's like for you. Because I know you think I don't have a learning disability, but I can't remember names worth a darn, or where we've been or what's been said—not like you can. But I want to know what it's like for you? Take me into that.

Buddy: I am relieved and I am proud. It's amazing to me that this is possible. You just skipped over the fact of my disability that's been on me forever and we're doing it anyway. So now I'm getting how capable I am in another way. When I was younger I knew I could present things, but the idea of writing a book—totally out of the realm. You've done a book before, so that's what made me say okay yes. I would go along for the ride. But that's not how it is. You never flinched. You just brought it out of me and now I feel we're equals in this and I never thought I would. In the beginning though, I was afraid.

Bob: I'm very touched. I wouldn't want it to be any other way but mutual and equal. It never occurred to me you couldn't do it. I'm used to seeing you knock 'em dead, be very with it, totally on target. And, uh, there's a way in which I can only imagine what it must be like to carry the fear of this thing around with you. Yet all during it, there's a way in which I don't know that anybody would ever know it's there. It occurs to me now . . . when I used to get irritated by your showing off, you know, the shining thing . . . getting the applause, what it's for. It's your cover. It's a pretty good cover. Not in a bad way but as an energy source, something that propels you through the fear.

Buddy: Hmmm . . . I don't know about that. I'm like a lot of other men in the sense that I don't know if I'd let a whole lot of people know of my struggle with the disability. It's not something I feel good about. I've worried about it a lot. But I believe you when you say people don't pick up on it. And it feels good right now to talk about it.

LEVEL IV: Communion

Level IV is an experience of friendship, loveship, companionship—a real sense of an opportunity to let it all hang out, to feel safe enough to expose our greatest joys, or weaknesses or sorrows, fears, and angers and to know that these will be met with interest and acceptance. It is a peak experience in relationship, a time when you really feel as if your soul is being understood and appreciated. In Level IV there is spontaneous physical contact—a touch of the arm or hand on shoulder, sometimes a hug or a holding of each other. Feelings prevail on Level IV. The exchange is mutual—back and forth—between both parties. Level IV is obviously not a place where people dwell for extended time, but rather one to reach for on occasion.

(Example of Level IV)

Buddy: What really bothers me is not the learning disability. It's that I can't stand to feel or appear inadequate,
not up to the job, not good enough . . . if I can't think
or describe things the way they are to me. This is what's
underneath it. Does that make sense?

Bob: Right, yeah, I have that too. When I talk about my
grandkids seeing this book, what I want is to be able to
let them know who their grandfather is. Who I am,
what I struggle with in my life, what I want in this
world. Right now I'm saying good-bye in many ways to
my own elderly parents and my wife's parents, so all
this is up close for me: how fast it all goes, what one
generation leaves the next, that kind of thing. Who
knows me? What have I contributed? Can I put it down
on paper . . . for the record? Will it be clear enough to
match what the work means to me? I'm wrestling with
this. Am I adequate to this enormous task? Like my
life's work! Am I up to it? It's scary.

Buddy: What does *adequate* mean to you here, Bob? I
mean, how might you be inadequate to the task? Tell
me.

Bob: Well, I have a learning disability too. Part of mine is
that I don't think I present myself verbally very well
and I have this tremendous need to make a statement
in writing that's clear. In some ways, I think we're two
sides of the same struggle. You with your dyslexia or
whatever it might be labeled technically, and me with
. . . for me it's like *bang,* here I am in the moment. Is it
going to come out right or am I going to embarrass
myself? I don't know . . . maybe it goes back to produc-
ing imperfect bowel movements . . . (*laughter*). Or
maybe the feeling is tied up with my flustered retorts to
my angry father when he was demanding answers and

all I could do was stammer. Or, you know who am I? I went a long time not knowing what I stood for, and then as I found my voice it got lost in the rumble of the sixties among thousands of voices, left me feeling insignificant. That's it, I want to make a statement that is unique, that is me, that is significant. I want to make a mark, a contribution that counts.

Buddy: So, yeah, it's different for me, but I hear you. And it's like underneath all this, what we're both afraid of is that we won't be loved, right? That's what it is, don't you think?

Bob: Sure. Okay, yeah. Good . . . all right, so then let me ask you. In all of this, in our writing and working partnership, what I want to know is, Buddy, do you feel loved by me? I know that I feel your love, your full acceptance of me when I struggle with the phrasing of something or whatever it is we've put ourselves to. Do you feel the same from me?

Buddy: Yes. Right now. And that's the greatest feeling. I do feel your love when I'm open to it. I feel your love, your presence, and your support. Yeah, definitely. So now my question is, will *they* feel it?

Bob: Well, here it is. This is a big part of it. I think what we want here is to lay the foundation for the reader to experience this, to have a relationship that puts his or her disabilities on the shelf. We've seen it done again and again face to face in The Men's Room experience. Now we want that to start happening with the book.

Buddy: Yes, that's what I want. Definitely.

And in the End . . .

Good, honest communication is one of the essential foundations of good relationship and good health. Nothing left lingering inside to knot up the neck, the belly, the fist, or the heart. The key to reaching any level of intimacy is to realize that you have the ability to get there. To realize this ability, you have to learn to notice on what level your interaction is taking place. If you remain aware of the level you are on, then you can take the conversation to whatever level you desire. The more we learn about how we speak and listen, the easier it gets to bring ourselves to people in a way that brings us naturally, consciously into relationship.

Timing and patience are key elements to intimate communication. Watch for the subtle cues in yourself and your partner. Often instead of listening to what the other person is saying, we begin at once to prepare our response. Good communication requires paying close attention to what is being said. When you notice yourself drifting, take responsibility to bring yourself back, regain your presence. It gets easier with practice.

The choice is ours. Sometimes we choose merely to continue to do the same thing that we've always done. Here we offer you and the men we see in organizations or in our offices the opportunity to learn a new language and style of communication. This means making effective choices— choices that will influence every relationship you have and also show you how to create the new relationships you desire. Before moving to the next chapter, let us say it again: If we always do what we've always done, we'll always get what we've always gotten.

FOUR

The Heart Beat

■ **We are sitting** in "the heart" of
The Men's Room, the center of the room where we began our
work with men ten years ago. It is empty now where we
are used to seeing 25–30 men in action. It reminds us of the
film, *The Graduate,* when Benjamin is waiting for Elaine next
to a fountain at the University of California in Berkeley.
Suddenly the classes let out and thousands of students pour
into the scene. This is the feeling we get when this room
fills up with the men who are beginning their journey in
The Men's Room.

> **BOB** ◆ For me the room is full. So full, it sends chills down
> my spine as I feel the energy and spirit, the pain, the ten-
> derness, remembering the events that occurred here—
> times when men jumped up, walked proudly, or sadly,
> torn inside out, into the middle of this room and began
> to address what was happening at the very core of their
> being.
>
> Right now, this day in 1995, the room is full of those
> moments and of these men. Their lives fill the space as the

two of us sit here together, as we have on so many occasions. Now we begin again the journey inward to the heart, to explore further with you what "heartwork" is about. There is a level of thriving, a quality of being alive that every man and every woman needs and can experience by taking the journey to the center of their being.

We start our journey into the heart today by reviewing where we've been and where we are. The day started at Northwestern University where we met to work out on the exercycle. While we pedaled we caught up on the news of last weekend's Men's Room which was led by two of the men we trained. Kevin Fitzpatrick and Paul Kachoris now co-lead a number of groups each year. Hearing their report of an exceptional weekend made us happy and proud. Every Men's Room weekend has its own identity, its own unique character, and we never tire of hearing how the work goes. It is always changing, finding new expression, new pathways in and out, and yet it is always the same profound awakening of spirit.

Exercising together has become a focal part of our relationship—a health ritual for body and heart, a time and platform for checking in with one another, discovery, a kind of mooring ourselves again in this place and time. There is a weaving of dialogue through the exercise as we look at where we've been, what we're thinking and feeling. The movement in and around deepens as we move closer to the heart. It begins as it probably does, with any couple or friendship in an exchange of information and then moves progressively toward the feelings—how we are impacted or changed, moved or sensitized by the separate events in our lives. The exercise, the movement, the activity becomes conducive to talking in a way that's different from just meeting over coffee. When men talk over their work or play, there is a distinct quality to the time. A rhythm is developed that cradles the relationship until a certain depth of connection is reached. It reminds us of the generations of men who hunted, foraged, and farmed together—coming out of themselves as they walked and talked and worked. ◆

There is a physical and spiritual component. The Chinese have done this for years in the slow body movement known as *Tai Chi* in which they both meditate for the soul and move for the body. We add talking and a new awareness of relationship to this ancient mix. It is not uncommon for our competitive instincts to emerge in this physical context. But as the conversation deepens and moves into areas of mutual concern, the competitive urge gives way to the more compelling dance of relationship.

Take a moment and think about the way in which you participate with others when you work out together or are involved in any activity. Are you aware of the urge to compete, to show your skill and superior abilities? Or do you fear you'll look worse? Does a constant comparison sap the pleasure you might get? These are our normal feelings. Only when we choose to do something different with the time, to bring something else into play, do we move beyond the competitive level of interaction into an entirely new arena of communication.

BUDDY ▼ Following the morning workout, we go to meet Bob's twin daughters, Claire and Tara, for breakfast. They are in town briefly between the end of spring semester at college and their summer jobs on the east coast. The ease, vitality, and energy with which these young women enter the restaurant is striking. Our corner of the room lights up with an animated, intelligent, humorous summary of their plans for study and travel, their assessments of "Mom and Dad's survival" without them, their readiness to pounce upon and examine closely any issue put forth. I am, frankly, thrilled to be here, a part of this family . . . and to know they are a part of mine.

As the executor to Bob's estate, I feel a deep sense of responsibility as well as the same father-pride that I feel toward my own children. As I alternately watch and participate in this unusual foursome, I am struck by the notion that few men today are allowed to feel this close to another man's children—as if they were my own. So that Bob's laughter and pride and obvious pleasure in his children's dexterity and depth of character is inseparable from my own. Would fathers fear for their daughters, as they do today, if these relationships were the norm? What if the role of father, for all of us, stretched beyond our immediate families and became a living support network for children everywhere? As I interact with these women and observe the powerful relationship they have with their father, and now with me, these thoughts tug at me. ▼

Heart Song

Do not mistake the word "heart" or "heartwork" for only the serious or painful. Although healing ourselves is a central focus, there is often, as in this meeting with our children, or in the center of The Men's Room a rumble of laughter, joy beyond reason, and a new-found energy that propels us right through the muck of everydayness. We share these stories with you as if to give you a tap on the shoulder, a time out to reconsider the possibilities, the knowledge that in learning how to be available, accessible to the people in your life—old and new—you become more and more who you are, how you are, only stronger, more confident, much happier.

As we return to the center together, the heart, you can see we have taken stock of our travels just today. The time we take for this inventory, no matter how brief, is essential. It is part of the preparation for us to enter the heartwork unfettered, complete, without a part of us still lingering in the play of conversation at breakfast. We take time to finish it up, to find closure, so the way is clear to take the next step.

Heartwork is always a surprise. We rise to it without thinking, because we are moved; and we intuitively or instinctively know it is time to come forward. Many a man has jumped up spontaneously, against his own desire to hold onto his seat, who was just one moment ago glued to his chair, but who suddenly finds himself standing in the middle of the room, ready to work. The work itself is in noticing and in speaking or acting out what has been noticed.

We remember Martin, standing in the center of the room knowing that cancer was eating away at him, knowing that his issue was to deal with the fear at the center of it. His desire was to own that fear and beat that fear. His goal was to discover how to live his life now, while he was still very much alive, and his intention was to stay alive as long as he lived rather than join the grave long before he was in it.

Ron, Larry, and Fred are men who in turn took their places at the center of the room to talk about their bodies—about being split in half. Ron is split down the middle; his left side belongs to his mother's Catholicism, his right side to the Judaism of his father. Ron is lost in the middle. Larry's split is between top and bottom. His top half knows radiance, sunshine, energy, excitement, but from the diaphragm down he feels a dark, evil, quicksand-like serpentine quality. Fred, keenly aware of two sides of him constantly pushing against each other, is another divided spirit.

The heartwork of these three men brings all of us together to face our ambivalence, our conflicts, and dualities. Standing in the heart, men face the fact that yes, there's a part of them that is this way, and another part that is different. The healing action in this heartwork has to do with acknowledgment and acceptance, with learning to let the fear out, to stop trying to crush and deny parts of ourselves that are begging to be known. We learn to let the tension express itself in our bodies, feel how it feels to us. When we do this together, with other men right in the ring at our side, our courage grows to meet the task. Traditionally, men have been taught to disassociate themselves (their souls) from the conflicts and fears they carry. The daily ritual of burying parts of ourselves in order to meet our obligations saps our vital energy, pulls us into a burial rite that can only yield up a half-life. When we turn to acknowledge and honor the parts of ourselves that we or someone else has found distasteful or wanting, we begin to make a shift toward reunion.

Other men erupt into the center of the room and are filled with a powerful, driving need to express themselves emotionally. Men who have kept their cool for a long long time. Like George, who wants to beat something to a pulp, to destroy it. He goes through the motions of this emotion until, to his amazement, he breaks through to an entirely different realm of feeling. Underneath the desire to destroy is an intense need to be comforted, to be held and reassured, to be praised, to be rewarded for behaving with courage. As he cuts to this new layer he begins to laugh and laugh. As the lightness of spirit overcomes him, you can almost see him flying around the room. And he does actually get up and leap, like the great ballet dancer Nureyev, in spins and elevations despite his squat, fire-plug body, twirling like a helicopter in joy.

The first feelings expressed as men come into the heart may simply be a mask for the feelings underneath, especially if the real feelings are perceived as unmanly, or weak. When we are taught that it is weak for a man to need comfort, he often resorts to anger to hold the real need in check, to keep it hidden—even from himself. The heartwork opens us to these secrets and, in doing so, helps to free everyone present.

As Stan begins his work he carries a gray cast, a pallor that comes from having carried so many loved ones to their graves. Stan needs to expel the grief over his father and several others he has lost in his life. The men invite his sorrow up into the room, and give him permission to let go of it, to bring it up for all of us to hold. When he completes his work, Stan is able to bury the gray gloves of a pall bearer who buried his father. The role play has touched all the men. Stan and the others can now watch a flower bloom or the sun set and not feel guilty with grief.

Jim finds himself in the center of the room, literally turning himself inside out in order to unearth a part of him that stands between him and all pleasure, all feeling. Until now, it is locked up inside him, so that when he looks at his wife or child he comes up blank. No feelings attached. His search yields up a deep slice of shame regarding a homosexual experience he and another boy had as children. He is able right here in the heart to be nurtured, re-fathered by the men in the room, in a way that allows him to finally let go of the shame. And when he starts to sob, it is from the joy of feelings he is beginning to regain.

The Cure

Heartwork is not a cure. These stories are not meant to be before-and-after shots. There is healing here and a beginning made by hundreds of men to move into their lives with an altered agenda, a new perspective on how they are put together, who they are, and where they want to go. Many men have experienced men's programs where the focal point is emotional discharge, where they go out into the woods, beat drums and chests, get out a lot of pent-up anger and confusion, achieve catharsis, and then return to life as is. Other men are directed by their communities or religions back into the family to be leaders and good role models. This may not be enough for many men. Our work is different.

Heartwork is applying the release of energy from expressed anger or sorrow directly to relationships. It involves learning how to make ourselves more available for the kind of intimate exchange that all humans need in order to be

healthy. In every case, the heartwork begins with acknowledging what is, and then moving forward to what can be. It
requires facing the dark shadowy parts of who we are as well
as those parts we habitually and more comfortably present to
the world.

It is not a cure for life but a celebration of it, the good
parts, the bad parts. The process is risky as well as exciting. It
moves the participant through a transformation that involves
self-revelation, self-acceptance, and gaining the ability to
experience other human beings as beloved and worthy of
respect.

Men who never sang a note stand in the middle of the
room and sing. Men who haven't been held since they were
babies, come into the lap in the center of the room, have
their backs rubbed, get held, comforted, touched non-sexu-
ally by hands that are there to soothe and heal. Men who
trust no one come to the center and allow themselves to fall
straight backward into the outstretched arms of twenty others who will catch them; the possibility of trust is born in a
world-leery man who for the first time relinquishes control
and allows himself to partake in a simple test of trust.

No one is forced or manipulated in any way to come into
the heart space to do the work. The experience is as strong
for those witnessing as it is for those ready to step into the
center. Some men find it easier to face the dark than others,
to come up against their fears, shame, regrets—the truth,
whatever it yields. The work allows men to enter deep
states of emotion on their own schedule, when they're ready.
Our job is to create a safe, challenging environment—a
container—that invites and supports everyone present to
begin the journey.

Respect

When a man moves to the center of the heart, others stand
in respect for the work that he's about to do. The work itself

is unique for each one who steps forward. More often than not it is transformative, moving from a core issue (often a place of pain) through various layers, cells of confinement, to freedom. Those in attendance plus the leaders help the heartworker to continue through the tough parts, the unknown parts, with many different kinds of encouragement, some physical and some verbal. When there is a breakthrough moment, the work is completed with a ceremony designed specifically for this man's work. This is followed by a proclamation by the heartworker, a statement of intention directed to what, where, and how he intends to carry the work forward in his life.

The circle of men who witness and contribute to the work will all experience the transformation personally on some level. Each pulls from the work an element that applies to his own life situation. Not every man will do a piece of heartwork in the center. Every man, however, has the privilege of being present and experiencing the transformation themselves. There is no escaping the touch of this profoundly personal work, and later on, each has the opportunity to contribute his own response to the work presented. This allows those who are shy or reticent in groups, or men who are simply not as ready as others, to participate fully at whatever level they choose. Men who are naturally very private have an opportunity not only to witness other men stepping outside of the usual barriers, but also to take this vision of another's insight and personal development back into their own lives. In turn, each man expresses his   appreciation for the hard work performed and one man's willingness to open doors for all the men present.

When the men begin to share what the work has meant to them, they often become very emotional. Of those watching, many cry. Yes, men cry at the pain and struggle of others. They cry as they identify with another's work, and their eyes fill with tears of joy at seeing another liberated from the shackles of the past. Men understand why the one standing next to them cannot express his feelings, and they rise to honor the fear, empathize with the vulnerability. As one participant said, "You'd have to be a stone to be here and not cry."

One Man's Issue

A major impact of the heartwork on all participants is the discovery of how similar men are, how common our ailments, fears, needs, confusions, complexes, pain, shame, joys, and sorrows are. Whether the concern is economics, health, relationship, or whatever, most men face the same issues. The key in helping men to health is in never shaming them about their level of participation in a process. Rather, they need to be encouraged to listen to others in a positive, supportive, nurturing manner, so that they can see how the work of others relates to their own lives. It is also vital for men to learn to notice how their bodies are responding to the work. A major goal is to reduce the shame that comes out of a competitive perspective of other men, and encourage men instead to discover the strong mentors and role models available to them.

Many men feel pushed by women to participate in groups that offer the opportunity for them to get free of some of their limitations, their self-containment, their lack of skill at relationship and communication. So when they first enter one program or another, they are very hesitant because the choice was not really theirs. It is important for women to urge men forward in these areas, but to do so in a positive supportive manner. Otherwise, men come into the group as if sentenced to an ordeal, and their availability and access to the work can be severely hampered.

The Beat Goes On

We'd like to invite you to come into the heart with us now

and witness some of the work. Before we begin, we want you to prepare yourself.

According to some spiritual traditions, the third eye, located in the middle of the forehead, allows us to see inside. And the third ear, inside the chest, enables us to hear what resonates deep within us. Try opening the third eye and using the third ear as you enter these stories. Pay attention to what's happening in your whole body. Notice the sensations.

Ron's Story

Ron is thirty-six years old, single, the eldest child of an interfaith marriage. His father is Jewish and his mother is Catholic. As a child, Ron tried very hard to please both his parents. He became Catholic for his mother and Jewish for his father. In the company of Catholics, he identified as such. With Jews, he was Jewish. In his mind these choices were necessary to win and keep each parent's love. But he also felt that these choices were on some level mutually exclusive. Thus he was continually torn between the two identities and afraid that at any time he might jeopardize the love of one parent or the other.

Ron's parents themselves had many unresolved issues, some of which were connected to their different religious beliefs. Ron's response was typical of many children. He absorbed his parents' unresolved conflicts as his own. As he grew from boy to man, the fear and confusion regarding his identity — religious, emotional, and psychological — persisted. He felt torn in opposing directions most of the time.

When Ron walked into the heart, the first thing he shared with the other men was a tremendous sadness over his inability to identify himself clearly as either a Jew or a Catholic. At this point a deep anger at his parents surfaced, as he felt the pull and push of each to accept and affiliate with one religious tradition over the other. Two of the men helped him express this anger by grabbing hold of both his arms and literally pulling him physically in opposite directions. This brought the rage out clean and clear in a place where it was finally safe to let it happen. He bellowed like a wounded bull as he pulled with all his might against his "tormentors."

Cleansed by this release, Ron then began to work at a deeper level, getting in touch now with his alienation from both parents . . . the cutting-off from them that was necessary when they were unable to resolve their own differences. This act of distancing oneself from the parents' unresolved issues is a common survival strategy of children. Although it gets us through a time of early conflict in our lives, it becomes increasingly dysfunctional as we move into adulthood. In our work with men over the years, we have seen many men discover internal conflicts in urgent need of resolution that stem directly from their parents' unresolved differences and open-ended conflicts.

The men who supported Ron through his heartwork were visibly, deeply touched. Many could relate to his fear and uncertainty, his ambivalence about who and what he really is. Ron came to the center of the heart with his anger and sadness and was greeted by men who understood the dilemma and showed him support and love as he wept and spoke of the pain of wanting the love of both parents. The men continued this journey with Ron as he realized, for the first time (despite several years of psychotherapy) that at thirty-six years of age he had systematically avoided any kind of long term, committed relationship with a woman. He saw this clearly now as the result of his fear of disapproval and rejection—a fear carried, religiously, from his early development into his adult years.

The meaning of this work centers around noticing and learning to recognize what interferes with our ability to be intimately involved. Ron completed this part of his heartwork in the following manner. We asked him to declare who he is now as a grown man, what identity he could embrace with regard to his religious orientation—one that he could be open about in all situations, without keeping one half of himself hidden. At this point, Ron asserted: "I am Catholic and I am Jewish. Together, a Catholic and a Jew, this is who I am." A remarkable and observable relief washed over Ron when he was able to make this statement—a relief that reverberated through the group as Ron's confidence rose to the resolution.

To acknowledge Ron's work and show our gratitude, the men present devised the following celebratory ceremony. One man from the group offered his services as rabbi and another as priest. The two "officials" conducted a very moving service to bless Ron in his decision to be of both his mother and his father. With the group as congregation, the priest and rabbi performed a Confirmation to honor Ron's Catholicism and a Bar Mitzvah to honor his passage into adulthood as a Jew.

This blessing for a newly anchored identity was heartily received by the entire congregation. For those who observed the ceremony, it brought up a strong reaction to the universal issue of identity formation. At this moment it was apparent to each of us that one man's issue is every man's issue, even though our stories are different.

Jerry's Story: *the Contained Bear*

It was Jerry's moment and he moved forcefully yet easily into the middle of the heart. He did so with a certain air of mystery and tension. Imagine a man about forty-nine years of age, 5' 11" who weighs in at about 175 pounds, pacing studiously, seriously, back and forth across the center of the heart. He is agitated. He is thinking . . . as if he doesn't know what to do next. He continues the pacing. We watch attentively. Gradually his looks start to change. His shoulders slope forward, a snout juts out, his arms hang out in front of him. As he continues to pace, we realize that he is no longer human; he is an animal of some kind.

We shout to him, "What kind of animal are you?" He growls back: "A bear!" So we say to him, "Keep pacing, Bear," and Bear continues to pace. With each passing moment he takes on more of the lumbering, muscular power of the bear, and yet, he also looks more and more frustrated . . . the pace takes on an angry edge.

"Where are you, Bear?" we ask. And he responds, "I'm in a cage," at which point almost without having to say a word, all twenty-five men who are present move in and become the squared-off cage. Our arms interlock and each of us becomes a bar of the cage. We instruct the bear to continue to pace. Bear continues to walk off the cage which now measures about 12' × 12'.

"Now, what do you want?" we ask. Bear is clear and quick to respond: "I want to break out of the cage."

"Then do it," we shout back. Bear rushes toward the bars, but the bars hold firm, and Bear rushes back to the other side and hits the bars full force, but they hold firm again. With each rush into the bars, Bear growls and becomes progressively frightened and wild. When he can't break through the bars, we offer him instruction on how to bring forth all of his power. The energy must come from the center of his being. To mobilize it, he will need to emit a great roar, so that the necessary force is created.

Bear roars and runs at the human cage again, but again it holds firm. But Bear does not give up. As the men try to hold him back, weeping and growling and fighting, he summons all his muscular and mental power to this effort. For a few seconds the room is filled with the grunts and sounds of man struggling against man in the contest between holding back and breaking out. Tears and agony from years pent-up inside come bursting forth as Bear finally breaks through the bars to freedom.

Then we ask him, "Where are you now, Bear?"

He answers, "I'm in the woods."

The other men rush to distribute themselves like trees in the woods and then we ask him, "What do you want in the woods?"

He responds: "To roam freely," and with that he lumbers through the woods, growling and roaming freely through the trees.

Soon enough he seems to tire of his freedom and begins to look very sad: a despairing bear all alone at the edge of the woods. So, we ask him, "What is the matter with you now, Bear?" and he says, through tender tears, the words contained for thirty years: "I am lonely. I need other bears." Now all the trees become bears and, because we are situated at our retreat site on a beautiful wooded peninsula in Lake Delavan, Wisconsin, we all move outside. Into the real woods we go, in the still of the night on a star-studded evening with a group of bears who proceed to follow Bear everywhere . . . and do whatever he does. His job now is to lead us in a joyful celebration of his freedom and his choice to end his isolation and move into relationship with others.

Off we run through the woods, around the trees, up the hill, down and around the buildings to settle finally at the edge of the lake where we have a full view of the moon and stars. And for the next half hour we silently observe what is inside and what is outside, as each man takes from the day and the moment what he alone needs most.

Holding this vision in your mind now, it would be useful for you to know that "contained bear" lost his father at an early age, that from the moment of his father's death, he built a wall around himself, a wall within which he confined his emotions and his freedom, his joy and his warmth, his fathering abilities and his passion. Finally, behind the wall he hid his ability to break out. All of this was contained within the wall that he built at the time of his father's death.

Despite an outwardly successful life, a wife, and several children, this man was isolated, this man was locked up inside himself.

Although many would have described Jerry as a very warm, lovable man, they also would say that he never quite reached out to others. And he could have told you that he never quite felt in contact with those around him, that there was always something holding him in check, keeping him caged.

Re-enacting the isolation, breaking through the cage, transforming his feelings into those of camaraderie and brotherhood, regaining the ability to play, Jerry is able to proclaim his new-found freedom and connection. This emergence from the containment of his own cave allows him to begin, and we mean *begin,* the process of developing authentic, unguarded relationships. For Jerry this will mean acting in ways that he has not been doing for nearly fifty years.

Jerry's break-through, if you will, by itself means little. The bigger picture centers now on Jerry's ability to develop a sense of what must be done to bring himself into relationship with others. He cannot allow himself to re-enter the cage that served him for years as a home (away from home) a protection from the vulnerability he felt as a ten-year-old child when his father died. This fear of being as vulnerable as we were as children is a major contributing factor to men's isolation and distance from others. It keeps us out of relationship and out of health.

For Jerry, a commitment to continue the journey of connectedness means that for the duration of his weekend he needs to notice and act upon those moments when he desires connection. He needs also to notice the moments of withdrawal, and to move actively into contact with others at these times. Over the course of the weekend he will have many opportunities to experience his new perspective. In order to feel secure in his freedom, he needs to put to use the knowledge that he can handle the emotions as an adult that were far too big for him to take on as a child.

This points to a major underlying cause of the men's movement: the tremendous hunger that men have to break out of isolation and move into healthy contact with people. The men who worked with Jerry on this particular weekend were made keenly aware of their own experience of containment through Jerry's heartwork. Each man could identify his own cell, his own containment. Through the metaphor and experience, each man could imagine the effort and direction needed to break out into life.

Sadly, we note that men often reject opportunities to come out of their isolation. One reason is because it comes to them in the form of criticism from women. Understandably, women become frustrated by men's withdrawal. They may ask the men in their lives, "What are you feeling?" They want to know why the man isn't talking to them, or they demand that the man get help. The problem is that for men there is an element of shame in these approaches. Sometimes men simply refuse to move forward in order to avoid further pain. Because of this we know that many men will miss out on experiencing the spontaneous break-through to contact that we see in every men's experiential weekend. Further, they will not get the immediate positive reinforcement of new behavior—so essential to making a permanent shift in their lives.

Buddy and Bob

As founders and continuing co-leaders of The Men's Room, it is essential that we practice the process that we teach to other men—not only for their benefit, but for health in our own lives. Also, we want to reinforce the notion that one does not arrive at any final point in heartwork. Like a river, heartwork is a powerful resource to be drawn from. But you can't get to the power if you don't go near the water. There is a necessary flow, a constant way of living with the work and working with our lives.

Buddy's Work

▼ It is mid-afternoon and I am aware that something is gnawing at me around the edges . . . throughout writing this chapter on heartwork. It concerns a conflict I am having with my wife. The conflict centers on issues of intimacy and closeness and how she and I approach these issues in very different ways. I am aware also that in the midst of my pain it is easy to feel that my approach is the right way, and hers is not.

Without going into the details of my marriage, which I consider to be a good one, I will tell you that the hunger I am experiencing is for more contact. The pain has to do with a feeling of loneliness, of being alone. In speaking of this now, I know also how many people who read it will nod in agreement, understanding that one of the most painful feelings one can encounter in an intimate relationship is to feel alone in spite of it.

For several hours now, I wanted to halt the writing and say Look, Bob, I have to talk to you about something. Now, I've decided this is a good opportunity to come out from behind the role of author and share myself as a man. Also, I believe that it is important for those of us who help people to health to do so through the example of our own work on ourselves.

The first question I am going to ask myself is, What am I doing or not doing in my relationship that is holding back the kind of closeness and intimacy that I crave? What is my part in the dilemma? What am I bringing into the arena of our differences that continues to get the kind of results that I'm getting? Because if you recall, if I always do what I've always done, I'll always get what I've always gotten. So I struggle now to understand what that might be.

What comes into my mind now is how critical I can be with my wife. In all likelihood, her interest and comfort in being an intimate partner with me, emotionally or sexually, may well be diminished by the amount of criticism that I bring into our relationship. It is, as I've mentioned, an easy voyage to self-righteousness to move my focus to my wife's part in the conflict. *But the power in heartwork resides in our ability to focus on what we ourselves bring to the table.* If I want to open up a way in for my wife I need to focus on being more supportive, warmer, loving, more forgiving in my approach to her. What goes around comes around. The more I am able to do this, the more available I will be for the kind of closeness I need to give and want to receive. A simple shift perhaps, but what blocks me entails a deeper look. How about you?

Looking deeper inside, I must also ask myself, What is it in me that wants to criticize my wife when I know that this will cause distance? Does it mean that somewhere in my heart I *want* the distance that I deplore? This is an important question, to which I have no answer right now. Heartwork does not yield up final answers. Heartwork is the process of developing good questions and the direction to work toward. My intention is to give this issue more thought over the next few days, to reach out and discuss it with my dear friend, Bob. He may well see some things that I cannot right now. I know that my marriage will improve when I do see what I'm missing right now.

My job for the moment is to do my own work. A good place to begin is to remind myself what a wise mentor of mine once said: "It's okay if you're critical, and it's okay if you're not." I am encouraged by these words to accept the critical parts of myself, rather than spending valuable time and energy on why I should or should not be who I obviously have been. Next, the phrase reminds me that I have a choice in the matter of what I will be now, how I will act in the present. Do I want the same or do I want something different? The choice is mine to make. ▼

Bob's Work

◆ For the duration of this chapter I have locked up my heart in order to focus on the cognition and logic of the writing. Opening it now, I get the image of termites scurrying out of a wooden ledge that has been tapped with a hammer. They run rampant, crazily, all over the place. This is how the heartwork feels to me at this moment. Just tapping that window sill with a hammer, opening the door to a flood of feelings, makes me well up with tears and puts a large lump in my throat.

I am a person in the middle. Looking in two different directions I see myself moving toward loss on both fronts. On the one hand, my mother is drawing closer to death as is my father-in-law who is a vital figure in my life. Both my father-in-law and my mother are in various states of physical and mental infirmity. On the other side of the age spectrum are my nineteen-year-old twin daughters who happen to be home for a week after their first year away at college. In only three days they are leaving for jobs in Massachusetts.

I look at this twin loss laying in wait for me and know that the closer I get to my loved ones the larger it looms. Part of me wants to push them away now, to save myself from the impact. Another part knows that having the contact gives me love from them that I need and also gives me the memories—many humorous and dear ones— but memories nonetheless that manifest in my heart now the impending wash of pain.

The bigger part of my heartwork is not knowing when and how to bring out these fears with my friends and with my wife. I worry of bleeding endlessly. Juxtaposed further is my maleness telling me to be strong and wear the pain in silence even though I know it is good to cry, human to be needy, wise to ask for comfort, and vital to be held and supported through crises.

I suspect I use these questions of when, where, and how much in order to avoid dealing with the loss directly. I am aware of a pain in my chest right now which tells me that this loss is very present for me and therefore needs attention. Although I've been dealing with it for a year now, it isn't through with me yet. The questions keep coming, and I continue to listen to my body for clues that indicate I haven't given it enough.

One day it will be enough. And right in this moment I'm aware that in the writing now I am getting some relief. Being here with my best friend Buddy is bringing me relief. Later in the day I'll bring this work home and talk about it to my wife. And when we have dinner with friends this evening it will come up again. I will allow myself to open the door, tap on the sill, and let the loss run around in its chaotic course. Only if I do this will I be able to relieve the pain in my chest and focus clearly on the work that will be in front of me tomorrow.

I am aware of the paradox of love and loss, of the duality of tears and laughter that surrounds each of these important people in my life. I like my ability to be in touch with these dualities. An important issue for men certainly, and for women as well, is the permission to be in touch with the duality of life, to not be in an "on" or "off" mode, to not have this world be just one color, to allow ourselves to hold both sides—love and loss, tears and laughter, anxiety and excitement. I notice how moving deeply into one side often allows me to come out on the other side.

As I hugged my daughters and kissed them good-bye this morning I felt a great joy and tremendous satisfaction in the depth of my relationship with each of them. I take great pride in seeing how successfully and beautifully they are in the world as adult women now. In the same moment I am in touch with how they are slipping through my fingers, heading off, not just to Massachusetts but into the rest of their lives. In this juxtaposition of pleasure and pain rests the essential duality of life and the meaning and sense of the paradox for me.

Several times my mother, sick with Alzheimer's disease, has expressed a desire to commit suicide, to end her own physical and mental anguish. When I follow through the steps she might take toward a suicide, reaching the point (I know would come) when she would not remember what it was she set out to do, I feel the horror of it right next to the irony and humor. In all of this I am blessed to possess the love that allows me to feel the pain. What I am most grateful for is that I know how to search inside for the feelings, to let them come in whatever form they will. In relationship with others I have the opportunity to turn this intensity over into a greater and more supportive arena than I could provide all by myself.

Within each of us, about almost anything of consequence, we can find a duality, an ambivalence, both sides now. Many of us hurry to decision, rush to conclusion. Exploring opposites, living in the time before decision or action is uncomfortable. Entering the avoided side raises anxiety. Our experience tells us, however, that going to the unexamined side, letting the feelings there form as sensations first, later speaking them, gives us a fuller, richer life and wiser choices. Take a few moments to reflect on how you've seen this work. Once engaged with heartwork, most of the men we've met choose to listen closely to what comes from within. ◆

FIVE

Forever in
Our Hearts

The Apple Does Not Fall Far from the Tree

BOB ◆ Two red foxes cavort across the open, manicured grounds of Shalom Memorial Park in Palatine, Illinois, oblivious to Buddy and me, who have just placed long-stemmed roses, one for each, on Buddy's father's grave and then on his Uncle Morry's. All the markers are flush with the earth, so the overall impression looking outward is light, expansive, even buoyant with the arrival of our unexpected guests. Only when the glance falls, do the shiny-faced headstones come into focus, like little patches of ice spread out to melt in the midday sun.

Two roses, two brothers-in-law, two friends, two foxes is a little too much even for Buddy and me who are, by training and trade, attuned to patterns of events that others may take as mere happenstance. As we peer at the roses, a moment or two of sheer expectation lingers while each of us wonders silently, What can be next? The foxes, of course, show up to honor camaraderie, simplicity, and all that is naturally playful among men. This scenario gives us pause to think about peers, about relationship, about sharing the simple things . . . and what all of this may mean to the sons of fathers anywhere.

When we began our work with men in 1984, on the first weekend we brought a single rose to occupy the stand between us. At the close of that weekend we designated one man to be the keeper of the rose for the whole group, a man whose work most closely represented all the men's work. Each subsequent group has had a keeper of the rose. Today we bring one rose for Buddy's father and one for Uncle Morry to honor each man's place in Buddy's heart. ◆

BUDDY ▼ In 1965 Uncle Morry dropped dead of a heart attack. He was forty-seven and I was seventeen. The loss was monumental, not just because I was crazy about him, but he was the first man in my life to show me I could be different from my father. Uncle Morry was single, witty, worldly wise, and the women liked him. In my family the story was, you could tell how many ladies were hovering near-by from the number of toothbrushes lined up in Uncle Morry's bathroom. The colors he preferred to offer his special friends were pink, blue, and yellow. In my mind, this was the coolest. He never bragged about it, quite the contrary, but in that neat row of pastel toothbrushes I saw a world of possibility. My father was sweet and self-effacing while Morry, my mother's brother, had a touch of arrogance and was tough. I never got away with any non-sense in Uncle Morry's presence. Without looking up from whatever he was doing he'd say, "Knock it off, pal," and that would be that. I idolized him. ▼

Dad Gone Blues are Killing Me

Over the past ten years we have met with a thousand sons who have lost their fathers in one form or another. To a man, no matter how angry or "finished" they were with this loss, each one of these sons was seeking some fathering for himself. Whether the loss is due to death, divorce, or diversion (the father has no time for the child), there is always a dying in the experience, and a healing required to mend it. Each loss affects directly every man's capacity to form and perform in relationship as an adult, and also each man's ability to father another.

BUDDY ▼ In my own case, I am reminded of the pain that I experienced as a twenty-one-year-old as my father was dying—ravaged by intestinal cancer. I had to leave Northern Illinois University and move back home to help my family, while I enrolled at the University of Illinois, Chicago campus, for seventeen credit hours each semester. To support myself I worked thirty-two hours a week at Forest Psychiatric hospital in Des Plaines, Illinois. My mother didn't drive and needed to be chauffeured to and from her job at Saks Fifth Avenue, to the hospital, to buy groceries, to run all the errands required to keep the household working. My father had a nephrostomy and the plastic bag he wore for collection of urine had to be emptied and cleaned regularly. I never questioned my role in it, which came as naturally as waking up in the morning. But the responsibility, the hours, the pace were relentless. Meanwhile, my dad was trying to get his business completed before he died.

One windy Friday afternoon late in March of 1970, I drive him to his accountant's office on the corner of Western and Lawrence on the north side of Chicago. Looking at him, slumped in the passenger seat next to me, sends a wave of anguish through me. He is down to 115 pounds and it is all he can do to remain upright as he clutches the fat sheath of tax papers he has worked on for days. Clipped to each of the manila file folders is a check made out to the IRS.

Thankfully there is a parking space in front of the building. As I help my father out of the car, the sheath slips and drops to the ground. Papers fly everywhere. He screams and grabs helplessly at the empty air in front of him. Carefully, I prop him against the side of the car and leap for the papers. One of the checks has slipped its clip and is cartwheeling down the middle of the street some thirty feet ahead of me. I dash after it, cars honking, my father screaming behind me: "Get it! Get it! Get it! Get it!"

A half a block away, I retrieve the check and run back to the car. When I get there my father, so gentle and soft-spoken all his life, grasps my sleeve and unleashes his rage: "You idiot, you fool, you goddamned good-for-nothing idiot! How could you be so stupid? You let the check go!" I am looking at this crazy man, my father, and I'm considering euthanasia . . . on the spot. Choking him right there in the street. The accountant comes rushing out of his office to see what the ruckus is about. Finally, we go inside and the business is completed.

When we are safely back in the car, I turn to my father and let him have it. I spend every ounce of energy unleashing my own rage and frustration, my total incredulity over his behavior, his complete lack of gratitude, his uncaring, blind, cruel, hideous treatment of me under the circumstances. I blow my top, all the pent-up everything pours out of me.

This episode comes back to me now in all its fury and horror. The devastation I felt over the incident was irretrievably galvanized by the impending loss. Raised to be a giver with a capital G, just like my father, there was a voice born in me that day that still to this day says, "Look at all I've done for you and what do I get?" I carry this attitude, this hurt and disappointment down under. It can resurface with a vengeance when I am faced with similar circumstances. There are even times when I set up circumstances that will give this darkness inside of me a voice.

The day after I turned twenty-two, my father died. He was fifty-two. This loss contributed much to my own development and specifically to my fathering. I am intense about health issues, mine and my family's, because I remember how young he was, and I recall how much I missed his presence when there was still so much to share with him. Throughout my early years my father used to say to me, "If only you would apply yourself, Buddy, everything would be all right." But I was restless and disinterested in academics or settling into serious career preparation. I was busy being young and having fun. By the time I graduated college, he was gone; it was too late for him to celebrate or share this milestone with me.

To sit here now as an adult male and to talk about the impact that my father's life and death had on my own, and to do this also with the memory of my Uncle Morry allows me a measure of what I missed with them. In this visit to the cemetery, in the remembrance, I am getting in touch not only with a flood of memories but with the power of the bond that unites us, despite their absence. ▼

BOB ◆ And I remember a time when the only recognition forthcoming from my father was stinging criticism or rage. When I was young and feeling insignificant, the one man whose applause I craved was impossible to approach. Caught in a maelstrom of frustration, I wished for his death almost every day.

I am thinking of this time and then the time when I was finally able to mobilize my anger and sadness, to give him back the truth. I was thirty-five years old before I could face him. I arranged to meet him for lunch in a very nice restaurant, explaining only that I had some personal business to discuss. I remember my mother tried to talk him out of coming that day. She was afraid as soon as she heard of the meeting, for she knew it meant trouble. He brushed her protests away, she was making mountains of mole hills, it's only a sit-down conversation with Robert.

At the restaurant he and I were seated next to the window. It was a lovely spring day. Everyone around us was chirping about the good weather, glad for the green and warmth at last. We ordered and exchanged small talk until the food arrived. I wasn't going to rush it. I was going to wait until I was ready. Halfway through the meal, he grinned at me through a mouthful of salad and asked casually what was on my mind. I stared at him for a moment as he finished chewing. I watched him swallow, and then I began in a voice I know well but seldom use. Through clenched teeth, in hushed tones, I quietly explained how ashamed and hurt I felt for as long as I could remember to be his son. "You are," I said, "the worst father any son could have had."

I did not know how he would respond . . . if he would start the bellowing in anger or what. I didn't care. I was completely focused on what I needed to say.

"Bobby, don't . . ." he started . . . but I continued and he fell into silence. Silent amazement. It was the first time in our lives that he really listened to me. And it is amazing how those with so-called uncontrollable tempers, such as my father, control their tempers readily given the right circumstances. Shazam, this was it. I let him know that I was done, that it was over, and if he wanted a relationship with me and my family (including his twin granddaughters) it was up to him, but I was not going to make it happen.

He looked at me and said: "You're right—everything you've said. I don't know if I can do it, but I'll work at it."

I let him know that I'd tell him when he was on target and when he was slipping. He'd have to do the rest. That was it—a new path. Another man's journey begun. My only regret was that it took so many years to realize such enormous relief.

A gradual evolution of our relationship followed. He learned to come to me and ask for information, ask genuinely and pleasantly for time with me and time with my family, discovering finally and acknowledging his need of me and his curiosity about my life and my work. In this shift a new relationship was born. Now, I am also acutely aware of his age, eighty-three, and the loss that is before me. ◆

We are struck by the number of men who have stories filled with sadness and anger about fatherless times, fatherless lives past. Some thirty men's weekends, countless hours of individual treatment with many additional hours spent working on ourselves, provide clear testimony to the loss, the anger and distrust, the idolization and mystification, the power and the weakness of the men we sons call father.

What Love's Got to Do with It

We need to be acknowledged by our fathers. Seeking this unique recognition drives us toward many achievements. Or, it can drive us to failure if we give in to the darkness and perceive that no matter what our accomplishment, the recognition we crave will never come. Our relationship with our fathers, be it good or bad, acknowledging or defeating, caring or indifferent, also plays a major role in our present relationships with others.

Once the rage and sadness are confronted and moved through, we face the harshest fact. While we may disdain the company of those whose footsteps we were born to follow, we are bound to fill the shoes. Here is where we come face to face with ourselves. Now we notice the depth of the charge, the strength of the impact. We identify with our fathers regardless of the nature of our relationship with them, no matter if they treat us with kindness or cruelty.

> **BOB** ◆ For a moment, think about how you are similar to your father, not so much in your behavior, but in the ways you think and feel, and in your attitudes toward people. Many of us wish to deny the similarity or the underlying connection to our fathers. I have certainly spent many years not being able to see any connection of substance. My father was considerably overweight, while I was thin. He was angry and I was gentle. He was explosive; I was patient. In my mind there could be no similarities. For a significant period of time in my life I was reasonably convinced that I was adopted.
>
> Then he had a heart attack and surgery. Forty pounds of accumulated fat was surgically removed. This was followed by a diet on which he dropped another fifty. One day I found myself watching him from the back, walking away from me and I said to myself, That's how I walk! With this awakening I began to realize that I not only walk like him, but talk like him. In complaining to my wife I heard the same pitch and tenor, the maniacal concern with detail with which I once watched my father torment my mother.
>
> Indeed, once I opened the door to them the similarities between my father and me seemed to march through it in numbers quite disturbing. The good news is that I began for the first time to be able to see in my father qualities I respected as well as those I could not stomach. With this recognition the wall of my own prejudice toward a father who had hurt me as a child could begin to come down. The blocks to my emerging relationship with my wife and children could also be removed. In this way I was able to leave behind me a script written by another. ◆

It is normal to remove connections that have lacerated the heart. Some men go to the grave denying the connection with their fathers, especially true when the fathers have been alcoholic or abusive. Similarly, the abandoned son will break the connection in his mind because to do otherwise is too painful. Then there are the fathers who were absent even while they were present, the fathers who simply tuned out of the fathering role in order to escape to higher ground. Sometimes the discovery period is hardest for sons of the latter because the disappearance is subtler. There are some others who, while they know their fathers loved them, have no memory of a hug, a touch, an I love you. This separation of physical and verbal expression from emotion can actually be one of the most difficult things for the child to surpass. Finally, there is the present but critical father who, although he genuinely wants the best for his children, invariably drives the children away emotionally.

All the men we see have, at one time or another, lost their fathers—either spiritually, emotionally, or physically. The first challenge is to loosen the emotional barrier that prevents them from seeing both positive and negative aspects of their identification with their fathers. The primary purpose of men getting to know about their fathers is to expand their understanding of themselves.

> BUDDY ▼ There are men, of course, who have loving, present, attentive fathers. I am aware of how gentle and loving my own father was. Yet he was also very hesitant to assert himself, to state his goals and desires and chase them down, to achieve what he wished for. I ask myself, What of this have I kept with me, how is it presently in my life, and how have I moved away from him in my pattern of living? Through this process I gain a conscious perspective and my own capacity to assert myself expands. ▼

Finding the Father at Home

The following stories of father/son heartwork out of a recent

Men's Room experiential weekend are typical. Carl was only twenty-four when he stepped into the heart to do his work. It was time, he said, to assert himself in his relationship with his father, to face him, to take issue with the pressure Carl was getting to move in a direction with which he was not personally comfortable. And he was afraid.

This fear for many men rests in the center of their heart and orchestrates much of the way in which they conduct their lives. The fear of losing father's approval and acceptance, the fear of being without the blessings that come with that acceptance is for many men primary.

To begin we instructed Carl to select a man from the group who would make a suitable role model as his father. He was also reminded to pay close attention to his body's response in making his choice. The selection of a role model is very important. Men choose other men to play their mothers, fathers, sisters, brothers, wives, sweethearts, daughters, and sons. There is a chemistry in the selection process that never misses. Those doing the work always seem to know who is the best candidate for this role. The selection is made silently from close observation of the prospects. We remind the men every time to pay attention to their body's response, because we believe the body knows more than we are conscious of; it's a matter of learning its language, letting in the signals.

Carl proceeds slowly around the circle. He stops and looks into each man's eyes as he goes. He notes their physique and his own response to their bodies as he searches for the connection. He hesitates in front of Mark, who is taller than Carl, and Carl also notes an arrogance in Mark's stance, a challenge in his look that suits him. "You will be my father," Carl says, nodding as he makes the selection. Mark steps confidently into the center of the heart with him. They stand and watch each other for a moment, taking a measure of who they are dealing with, getting ready for the dialogue.

Carl: I'd like to have a talk with you, Dad.

Mark/Dad: Fine, son. Anytime. What's on your mind?

Carl: I know it's important to you that I make a decision about my career. And I know you hope that my decision will be law or engineering, but . . . well, I . . . I don't want to go into either law or engineering, and at this point . . . I'm not quite sure what it is I want to do. I feel like I haven't looked around enough.

Mark: You say you want to have a talk, but it sounds to me like you don't know what you're talking about. I mean, I've suggested law or engineering as two realistic alternatives. You have a good background for either one, and well, that's where I've got good contacts for you. What's the problem?

Carl: Well, like I was saying, the problem is I don't think I'll be happy in law or engineering. And I think this is a decision that I need to make for myself, you know, be sure myself of where I'm headed.

Mark: Well, son, let's face it, you're headed nowhere right now. You've gotta get realistic about this; you're no college freshman. You're out and about now. It's time. Hell, it's past time. You think another year of wandering in circles is going to steer you right? Just give me the benefit of the doubt here. What's wrong with law or engineering? I've been in both fields for nearly thirty years. I know what I'm talking about. And I've about had it with your indecision.

At this point Carl starts to get very angry at his father. We encourage him to go deeper. Get into it as far as he can, pull out the stops. Not to injure the father, but because the anger will mobilize his energy, help him through his block to speaking his heart, help him to stand his ground and assert his independence.

Carl, like many men, feels smaller than his father. As he gets larger, he can risk the anger, the offense. He is growing big enough in his own feelings to risk the current relationship he has with his father, to stimulate it to move to a new place. His anger fuels the journey to higher ground. When his father finally falls silent in the exchange, and the anger is still high but has no where in particular to go, Carl begins to move into other feelings. He becomes sad, nearly despairing, as if he has imploded.

For the reaction to be so swift there must be a resonance to reality here. Carl's father may withdraw from anger, from understanding the impasse, or for some other reason. The father's motivation is not important now. Carl's response is. As Carl feels the father backing off, he comes face to face with his own stake in the old relationship, the dependency. We are asking him now, "What is the sadness about? What are you feeling? Where are you in your body? What do you want?" Carl says he is afraid of losing his father. Moving through the sadness he realizes now that the reason he has postponed this exchange is not only due to his father's need to maintain the parent-child interaction, but also Carl begins to recognize his own need. Leaving one foot in dependency had reassured him that he would not have to go on alone. The dependency itself represented a loving, intimate relationship with his father that he did not want to lose under any circumstances.

Men commonly have this kind of relationship with their fathers. They need the father's guidance and blessing, not because they're unable to make their own decisions and determine their own path, but because this is the way they feel they can maintain the love and closeness they felt—to a greater or lesser degree—at an earlier time in their development. Men are in conflict over how they can maintain or develop a loving relationship with the father and also be independent.

Akin to the dependency conflict is one which is experienced by men who lose their fathers through disease, death, divorce, or diversion. This loss comes at a time in life when the child needs guidance, spiritual, emotional, cognitive guidance. Bear in mind the "child" can be of any age. Because a man turns fifty does not mean he enters a magic realm where guidance and advice is no longer needed.

When Wayne was ten years old his parents divorced. His father moved away and broke all contact with his ex-wife and son. Wayne is thirty-five years old when he comes into the heart. He is struggling to make his marriage work, and his career situation is uncertain. He doesn't know whether to leave the firm or stay and aim for partnership. He is experiencing overwhelming feelings of emptiness, of not knowing what he is supposed to do with his life. He wants advice, guidance, feedback, input from someone who understands, who gives a damn, who won't make him feel ashamed in his quandary.

Wayne selects a man named Ben to play the role of his father for the heartwork. We then ask Wayne to leave the room and prepare himself for the exchange by getting quiet and letting himself be with the frustration, the not knowing, the pain of an intense and unfulfilled need. He is instructed to consider his feelings for his father whom he hasn't seen in twenty-five years, to prepare himself for a reunion with this man. What does he want to say? What are his questions?

When he returns to the room we have the "father" seated on an elevated platform as if he were a king among kings. The other men form a reception line, leading to the "throne." Tears well up in Wayne's eyes the moment he re-enters the room.

This is not unusual, by the way. It may be difficult for you to grasp how realistic these heart vignettes become for the participants. In some ways, it's "more real," than it might be in real life because, unlike real life, we create in the heart a genuinely safe place for feelings to emerge. If he can't get at the feelings, the participant cannot move through them to another level of understanding, cannot reach the point where he experiences his own abilities and resources.

In real life the participant may not feel safe enough to allow the feelings to come. What we've learned over the years is that "safe" is an attitude, actually a portable attitude. Experienced in one place, it can be internalized, and taken elsewhere. This isn't exactly news, but sometimes we need reminding. Self-confidence is *self*-confidence—not something that comes from others. But it is built and practiced in an arena with others. If one misses out on the early "safe place" (where the child is accepted and loved regardless of his performance), this can cripple his sense of self and ability to take risks.

The safe place we create in heartwork serves two important functions: (1) It allows feelings to surface that might otherwise remain buried under layers of protection—feelings that teach us who we are and where we are, and (2) It provides a place where as adults we can practice and cultivate an attitude that escaped us in childhood. A sense of safety allows us time to slow down, time to sense, then talk in imperfect ways, flounder, say things we may even disagree with after they're spoken. It is a place where speaking our uncertainty or correcting our conclusions leads to growth, not to shame.

Wayne moves up the aisle formed by the two rows of men, stands before his father and says: "I have come to you for advice, father." The father nods yes. "I am feeling overwhelmed and uncertain about many things," Wayne continues. "I need your help in figuring out what to do now."

In a very loving way, the father responds, "Son, you must listen to yourself. You must stay in touch with how you truly feel, and you must do what your own heart directs you to do."

The tears begin to roll down Wayne's cheeks as he hears his father speak, and then he breaks into a full sobbing. When he is able to compose himself a little, he asks, "Why did you leave me?"

The father responds, "I had to follow my heart . . . although it cost me dearly, and gave me more pain than I ever knew before. It was not an easy choice, but at the time it was the only thing for me to do. I understand how much it hurt you and I am so sorry for that."

When the conversation between father and son is finished, they exchange formal good-byes. But the work is not finished. The father steps down from the platform and Wayne is asked to take up his position in the elevated chair. For Wayne to internalize what he has experienced (risking himself, proceeding successfully through immense uncertainty) he needs next to become a father to others. The other men line up and one by one approach the chair with questions they want to have answered. Wayne considers each man's question thoughtfully, and answers from the heart. In this last step he comes full circle and gains immediate reinforcement from experiencing the other half of the father/son equation.

In order to resolve the dilemmas and conflicts born of their first relationship with a man, usually their fathers, men as adults need to form substantial relationships with other men. This does not mean replacing bad fathering with good friendship, but rather it is an avenue for them to open their hearts and take the best a relationship offers. Doing so not only decreases the chronic isolation from which men suffer, it also gives them a foundation for building intimate, authentic nourishing relationships with others—their wives, their children, the people in their work lives.

Men who were fathered by self-confident, open, loving men—kind, considerate, concerned, and involved—perhaps those who regularly attended Little League or school events, have another point of view. When Tom first spoke up he stated: "I feel for all you guys who missed out on a good father, but that is not my experience." For the duration of our time together he was an enthusiastic and self-confident participant. But in the waning moments of the weekend Tom mentioned that while his father was there for him in countless ways, Tom had never been hugged or touched by his father, nor had they ever exchanged the words, I love you. Tom discovered that acknowledged, expressed love between men was . . . well, prohibited in his family. Even though he had indeed experienced strong fathering, there was something missing.

Before he left, he decided to visit his father on the way home, and speak to this issue directly with him. When he arrived he told his father that he needed him to be able to look him in the eye and say, "I love you." And he needed to be able to open his arms to his father and give and take the physical expression of that love. In a follow-up meeting with his group, Tom reported that the exchange with his father had been pivotal. Not only did it bring his father closer to him, a closeness that the father seemed to delight in, but also Tom felt he could now more easily ask of others what he felt he needed from them.

Forever in Our Hearts

BOB ◆ On the headstone to our left, I glance down and read these words:

SIMON EUGENE BERNSTEIN

1896–1986

FOREVER IN OUR HEARTS

I tap Buddy on the shoulder and point to it. Minutes go by in silence as we each play mentally with this simple and incredibly appropriate message. Finally, it comes to me. I turn to Buddy and ask, "Do you know what that is?"

Buddy answers somberly, "A gift."

"But do you know what it's for?" I press him further, anxious to announce my own conclusion.

"It's the new title for this chapter," Buddy whispers, perfectly straight-faced.

And I look at him, as I have looked at him on many occasions for the past ten years, as if I am seeing him now clearly, for the first time. "How did you know?" I ask, incredulous.

"For the same reason you did, I guess," he answers with a grin. ◆

At the center of every man's heart is a feeling for and about father, the one he has, the one he never really knew, or the one that got away altogether. Wrapped around the center is the love or the pain we must break through in order to get to our own unique sense of the father within, the one who is forever in our hearts. Here in the center is the kernel of our selfhood which harbors, among other things, an original source of life energy, access to whatever we require to move out into life and get on with it full tilt.

Upon Leaving Hallowed Ground

BOB ◆ Driving back to the city we begin to sum up our mood and reflections on this chapter on fathers and sons, a journey into our own histories in the making. To our surprise we harbor very different emotions about the experience. Buddy is elated. He has a distinct sense of completion, a feeling that any man who reads the work will take something of value from it into his own life. I don't disagree with him but on the other hand, I feel sad, anxious, as if much has been stirred but nothing put to rest and the only completion to be had lies ahead of me—vague, ill-defined, unspeakable in part. ◆

BUDDY ▼ For a moment here Bob has lost sight of the duality—of the excitement he has coming to him from the unknown, the joy of reunion he will experience when he sees his daughters again after a summer's absence, of the relief that awaits him when the lives of his mother, his father, and his esteemed father-in-law are finished with this phase and they are at last at rest. I acknowledge his pain . . . I also chide him a bit on the joyful aspects of cemetery living. Humor is the most direct route to the perspective that duality brings, to knowing in the moment that pain is the porthole to pleasure. ▼

Fathering Forever

Whenever men experience loss, real loss, it is common for confusion to follow. This is a result of the inevitable dialogue between heart and head as we strive to make sense of our experience. There is also between father and son an inevitable sense of incompleteness, perhaps integral to all significant relationships, as if they were stories permanently in progress. For such is the case. Even when someone who is part of us dies, as long as we persist, so do they. Most of us have experienced a new way of looking at someone long after this person has moved out of the center of our lives. And this is the point, the insights keep coming, if we let them, and if they are important to us. As for our current relationships these too are in motion and changing, works in progress, indeed. If we would influence the rate and direction of a relationship, we need to recognize who we are in it.

In this chapter we have attempted to show you a variety of approaches to the father/son axis in hopes that you might discover a part of yourself and your own father or fathering here. The term "fathering" in itself is meaningless except for its sexual, biological, and genetic infrastructure. Fathering as social reality, as psychological, emotional, and spiritual action has a history as complex and varied as man's own. If we want to extricate ourselves from the unconscious march of time, place, and circumstance that so clearly influences how our fathering unfolds, we need to understand ourselves and the fathering better.

The ground covered in this chapter is intended to be explorative rather than definitive. Our own understanding of the work changes continually and with every new group of men we learn more. We do not mean either to neglect the impact of women and mothers on men. Rather, we set out to examine specifically how our fathers not only influence who and how we are, but continue to affect who we will become. Only if we absorb the impact of the fathering we have known, examine it, and come to a new understanding of it, are we as free as we can be to move in a direction that is of our own desire and making.

There is an urgency we both feel for men individually and collectively to re-define and re-direct the role of fatherhood in society, specifically for the need and benefit of all the children. To move beyond the mistakes of the past we need first to embrace the roots of our present condition and decide where we want to be. If we want to move the apples we have to replant the tree. It is our intention in the next chapter to show how this task of moving the roots and replanting ourselves can be hastened, directed, and enhanced through the use of guided imagery.

Visualizing the desired experiences can move what has become entrenched. This is true whether rescripting past events to end as you'd wished or creating wonderful current scenes that open you to new possibilities—vistas different from all your past experience—or deeply felt adventures.

SIX

Man Does What
Man Has to Do

Caving in

In the first part of this chapter, join Bob Mark on a recent journey into his own work, where he meets the challenge of re-working a part of his personal history. For the next ten to fifteen minutes, free yourself emotionally and physically from other concerns. If there is a call you need to make, a chore waiting, or anything else you need to be involved with, go ahead and do it. Get it out of the way. Be sure there are no radios or TVs, family members, friends, or phone calls to interrupt you. It is important for you to get clear.

> **BOB** ◆ As explained earlier in the book, my daughters came home from college in mid-May, and after a short re-spite, a refueling of sorts, they resumed their new lives away from their birth home and from me and my wife. I've also mentioned the gradual weakening (and disappear-ance in effect) of my parents due to illness and old age. By

July the combined impact of this transition sunk in and I slid into an unprecedented *malaise.*

Each day it got harder to get out of bed. Once I dragged myself to the shower, there was no point in getting out. The thought of cutting the hairs on my face felt cruel. The space I moved through filled up with molasses. Once upon a time each client who walked into my office appeared as a unique and lovable challenge. Now I opened the door to an endless line of troubled tin soldiers. I looked at my day's work and blind repetition stared back at me. The corners of my eyes and mouth bowed. Just underneath my skin across the bridge of my nose the tears formed and slid down the inside of my cheeks. I was going numb. My wife would ask me to pick up something on my way home and I'd forget it. Days passed without my having the slightest urge to call Buddy. I was not only alone in these feelings, I wanted to be alone in them.

One sunny Sunday morning I found my way out to the double swing in our back yard. Swaying listlessly back and forth, I watched my wife work in the garden. I thought of joining her and dismissed the idea. The newspaper lay unopened on the porch. I hadn't exercised in days, weeks possibly. I was just sitting there . . . an old man on a swing. All of a sudden my wife appeared in front of me. "What is *wrong* with you?" she asked.

I looked at her for a moment and out of my daze I answered, "My life is over." I vaguely expected an argument from her, exhortations to consider my enviable professional success, my beautiful children, my sailboat, but no. My wife, also a clinician, stared at me for a moment longer and said: "You are not qualified to treat yourself, nor am I." Only then did I admit to myself that I might need help.

I used the two-hour drive to my therapist's office to pry deeper into the root of the depression. I knew when it started. I knew what triggered it. The symptoms were common enough. But I knew also that by penetrating the topsoil, going for the darker stuff underneath, I could make better use of the hour to come. What came up for me almost immediately was the sense that something fundamental was missing, not so much a loss (as in impending loss of parents and loss of grown children, etc.) as I thought, but there was something not there, a black hole, a space unaccounted for in my life. It was a feeling I'd had before.

Driving this stretch of interstate highway, the feeling started to come back in the form of a sadness I felt years ago when I first discovered the little boy inside of me who got ditched along the way, whose parents gave him up to the world a little too soon, before they ever had an inkling of who was in there. Here he is again, sitting on a rock all alone by the side of the road. The kid is sad. Makes me sad to look at him, sitting there all by himself in the middle of nowhere. So I pull up to the side of the road and say to him "C'mon, kid, we're taking a little trip to Milwaukee. Hop in." He looks up at me with eyes that could break your heart. Wordlessly, he opens the door, climbs up on the seat, folds his arms across his chest, and looks straight ahead. I reach across him to pull the door shut and off we go. Me and the kid—both of us sad now right alongside of each other. For a minute or so I try to cheer him up. I tell him how glorious it is to be alive, all the incredible things that are in front of him. But it's useless, he's gone, down for the count, inconsolable.

On we ride in silence. And into this space, this emptiness between us in the car and outside of us on the road, in this time before time after time, it occurs to me that I cannot go back and introduce this child to his mother and father, anymore than I can introduce myself to them, or all that I have known as a grown man. I cannot even take this child by the hand and introduce him to my daughters, who are much older than he is and really not interested right now in little boys. They would not have time for him. They will never love him as he is. And it seems to me now that those closest to my heart will forever be out of reach of an important part of who I am. It is too late.

By the time we get to Milwaukee I am fully into my funk, although I smile at the thought of Dick Olney's large frame and knowing smile lumbering past the receptionist to greet me. Dick is one of the few beloved mentors in my life. At seventy-nine he has slowed a little, yet he keeps the schedule of an ambitious man in his prime. I am lucky to find him in town for he is on the road lecturing, presenting papers, giving workshops and seminars year-round in addition to his private clinical practice.

His background and training are eclectic and unorthodox. In practice he draws from theology, the arts, especially poetry, as well as philosophy and psychology, winding his way facilely from Plato to Gurdjieff to William Blake to any number of present and past Native American shamans with whom he has studied and prayed.

One might mistake Dick's casual rumpled attire and longish slightly mussed hair for a countercultural fashion statement. To the contrary, it is merely the result of a complete disinterest in personal exhibition or amplification. His focus is exclusively internal and otherworldly. Indeed, he deplores what he calls the "pseudo spiritualism" of the New Age movement. This confuses some of his most ardent students who are as apt as any to lump him in with any number of make-over gurus. He doesn't buy it, even if he shares a certain sage eccentricity with some of them. In any case, I give myself over to this unusual ministry as I have on occasion for the past six years, confident the time will be richly spent, regardless of how far I have fallen from the moment's grace.

His inner office is cavelike and cozy—small, roundish, the dimensions top to bottom about equal to the width and depth of the room. Artwork from around the world and several different centuries decks the walls. Save for leg room, the furniture—four low-riding overstuffed arm chairs snuggled into the corners—fills the space. Drums and various other percussion and wind instruments are strewn about, with a couple within easy reach of his own chair.

"Good to see you, my friend," he says in his quiet baritone, seeming not unlike Chief Sitting Bull beckoning a distant relative into his tipi. As I look into his dark watery eyes, it occurs to me once again how old he is. I never retain the thought because everything else about him is so permanently playful, spirited—immortal, actually. Although I am treading the depths of a significant depression, I feel lighter already. Being with Dick is for me tantamount to crawling up into the lap of a large and generous great-grandfather, or great-grandmother, for he has reached an age where neither the masculine nor feminine predominate.

He begins as he always does, nodding and asking, "Do you want to work today?" Dick doesn't call his sessions sessions or therapy. To him it is work, in the best sense of the word: consuming, challenging, creative, and deeply satisfying.

"Yes," I answer, "I am here to work."

"So what will it be today?" he asks, as if we are making a selection from a menu at the local diner.

I tell him of my recent plunge, of my parents' growing feebleness, of my children leaving home again, and I speak of how the road before me is gray without mercy, endless.

"My life is over," I conclude dramatically, feeling my words are not one jot exaggerated or overstated, feeling, yes, my life is over. It is an enormous relief to say it now to Dick.

"I see," he says. And unlike many a clinician faced with a depressive client, I believe Dick does actually see. You can almost see him see. He takes me in . . . in a long, steady gaze that lasts several seconds, and then a little smile flickers across his face as he leans toward me and whispers. "Perhaps it would be helpful for you, Bob, to exchange 'My' with 'That.' It's minor, of course," he continues, "but . . . it could be a little different for you with 'that' instead of 'my.' "

I remember thinking, What is he talking about? I'm missing something here and at the same time I'm trying out, out loud, what I've heard. "That life is over." "That life is over," I say it again, eyes moistening. "That life is over," I do it a third time and the new phrase begins to sink in.

"That's right," Dick interjects quietly. "That life is over, so this one can begin. Endings and beginnings go together," he adds casually. "Have you noticed?"

"Yes, I've noticed," I say and I start to chuckle, tears now coming. Dick chuckles with me and this makes me start to laugh. "So," he interjects again, shaking his hand in the air for punctuation, "Let's take a peek at what's beginning for you? Shall we?"

"Yes, yes, yes," I repeat the word and feel this stuff . . . what is it . . . *excitement!* bubbling up from my bowels, the first in weeks, months, who knows? And now the tears flow, rolling down the outside of my cheeks, as I think silently to myself, "The guy's a genius, there oughta be a shrine." And I laugh out loud at the silliness of my thought of building a shrine for someone who's still so lively.

Meanwhile, Dick is moving along, and quickly I gather up the loose ends of my attention to catch up with him.

He has closed his eyes and is humming something barely audible. I watch him like a hawk now, so as not to miss anything, and I am straining to hear the tune he hums.

"Close your eyes," he cautions me, as if he were watching me watch him right through his own closed lids. "Close your eyes now, and breathe and relax. Good." he says. "Now I want you to go somewhere, just go ahead and go wherever you like. It's not important where exactly." I begin to breathe deeply and rest . . . and then I get an image of myself sitting on the bank of a good-sized river which is running the length of a valley. Across the river, looking up, are foothills with majestic brown and purple mountains rising behind them. The rays of the sun are making silver flashes bounce off the water and it is beautiful here.

I hear Dick ask, "Where are you?" and I tell him. "Look up in the sky," he says, "What do you see, what color is the sky?" I tell him the sky is blue. "Good," he says, "Breathe in the blue sky." I breathe in the blue sky. "Okay," he says, "What do you see now, what's happening?"

"Well, let's see," I say, "Umm, oh . . . there's a beam of light coming down from the sun."

"Oh?" says Dick. "Keep looking at the beam of light. What's happening with it?"

Way up toward the sun, there is something going on. I can't quite make it out, except it doesn't hurt my eyes to look right at it, and then I see a man, looks like a Greek or Nordic God, dressed in a rough-hewn toga of sorts. He is muscular with dark curly hair and he is sliding toward me down the beam of light. I tell Dick what he looks like and Dick asks, "Who is it, Bob?" I don't know who it is but I ask him, and without words or sound, he tells me his name is Thor. I relate this to Dick, who says: "Are you sure that it isn't Apollo? He looks like Apollo to me."

"No," I tell him. "It's Thor."

"Oh, okay," says Dick. "I just thought it might be Apollo."

I tell Dick that Thor is signaling me to follow him. "Go," says Dick, "Go, go, stay with him." Thor turns and runs into the foothills. I leap to my feet, wade across the waist-deep river, and scramble up into the hills in pursuit. Then he turns round again, and waves me on, as if to say, "Hurry up!" I join him as he starts up the steep rocky incline of the mountain itself. I am afraid at first because we are traveling so fast, almost straight up, but Thor laughs and reassures me, as the rocks roll down the mountain in our wake. "We cannot fall," he shouts back over his shoulder. "And if we do, think of the fun we'll have!" At this I feel a surge of strength and energy, and all fear leaves me, as we climb rapidly upward.

Suddenly, Thor disappears. I look around frantically for him, but he is gone. As I pull myself up on a ledge over head, I find the mouth to a huge cave. I think, Aha!, Thor has gone into the cave, and I follow. Inside the first chamber it is completely dark. A darker dark than I have seen before. Thick, pitch-black with no light penetrating from the entrance. I stop in my tracks and listen. Then I see them. Studded into the walls of the cave are thousands of the most beautiful translucent, sparkling turquoise gems. I am astounded at the sight and cannot think for the brilliance and cannot understand how I can see them glittering in so black a place, but I can. Then I spot Thor. He signals me to follow him further. We run through chamber after chamber, headed directly into the bowels of the mountain. In each new chamber the walls are covered with different colored gems—agate, emerald, ruby, tourmaline. We race onward through them all. Euphoria spreads throughout my body.

All at once we burst into a crystal room. It is as if this chamber is carved out of a gigantic diamond. We are surrounded by bright white light. The crystal walls are mutating into an ever changing array of colors like a kaleidoscope, to spectacular effect. I am in awe, standing in the center of this blinding, changing light field of energy. Thor signals me to stand still. When my heart stops pounding and I am quiet, I sense the presence of three additional entities.

One of them steps out of the shadows. She is beautiful—tall, lean, muscular, but her manner is gentle. She wants something from me . . . I can't tell what. She holds her hand out to me, beckons me to her. My human male energy responds and I move toward her, for what I'm not sure. I don't know if she will take me to her breast or if I am to have sexual intercourse with her. Whatever she wants I feel willing, eager. But as I approach I sense she has information for me—not mothering, not sex, just information. She is completely welcoming, though, and I approach her easily as she reaches for my hand.

Suddenly I am full of questions. "Who are you? What are you here for? Who is Thor? What new life am I beginning?" Her beauty overwhelms me, and for several moments I am transfixed.

Finally she speaks and, to the best of my recollection, these are the words: "I sent Thor to you. He is your guide for the adventure ahead. The energy you feel now is from Thor who brings stamina and courage to those who seek the distance. Your work is not over yet, nor your pain. But in all of it there is healing. The territory ahead is as vast as what is behind, and as before, it holds more questions than answers."

As soon as she is finished speaking, I know it is time for me to go. I have not greeted nor been greeted by the other entities who remain in the shadows. I sense they will come forward in the future. As I turn to leave I feel her step into me from behind, as if she were coming along for the ride. I whirl around to catch a glimpse, but all I can see is my own reflection in the changing colors of the diamond walls. The echo of Thor's hardy laugh brings me to attention. I can feel the warmth and humor of his invitation as we clamor back through the many chambers of the cave.

Reaching the entrance, we leap into the light and bound down the mountain together. I arrive at the starting point breathless, just in time to hear Dick asking: "Who is the woman?" I am able to tell him now that it is the feminine in me, my anima, in Jung's terms. Always able to feel intensely, be vulnerable, and "minister" to others, I know that my feminine side is well-developed. Now it appears I am ready to explore the masculine, denied until now because as a child I could not help but equate it with my father's anguish and emotional brutality.

"Good," says Dick. "Then let us finish with this last piece, are you ready?"

"Fine," I tell him, "What do you suggest?"

Dick instructs me to invoke an image of my mother and father, running down a road. I start to laugh because I never saw them run before. For a moment then I am stunned by its vividness, its clarity of detail. Sometimes on these journeys that I take with Dick's guidance, the image is less compelling. When the image is strong, however, it evolves under its own steam and I can step out of the way to observe.

Now I see that my father is several yards ahead of my mother and moving in a giant lope, a lopsided galloping motion in order to carry the extra weight. In this image his bulk and fat are even greater than they were when I was a boy. As he lopes from side to side, the weight sloshes back and forth with each stride, like water over the edge of a bucket in motion. Watching him I get seasick, the nausea overwhelms me. I am aware of being completely separate from him. My mother darts along behind him in tiny little steps as if her feet were bound at the ankles. Nonetheless she is running hard because if she doesn't keep pace, he will die. I feel like turning away, but feel myself stuck in the same way she is as I watch them struggle onward.

Dick asks me to look at their faces. An angry grimace is frozen over my father's face and my mother looks terribly frightened and tense. I am amazed now to realize how much of my life these expressions represent, how clearly I carry them with me today.

Dick tells me to change the image, to place them side by side, facing me. Then he directs me to carefully, without hurting them, open their chests to see what is inside. Gently, carefully, I open each of their chests, rather like opening an *armoire*. Looking inside my mother, I am startled to find her heart the size of an almond. In fact it has ripples in it like an almond. It looks very hard and small. But inside my father's chest is a huge heart—bright red on the outside and black on the inside.

Dick suggests that I reach inside and touch both hearts. As I reach into my father's heart I am surprised to discover that the red is an acrylic paint, covering an outer plastic shell. On the inside, the blackness is a thick fur-like velour that is warm and moist, quite inviting and very pleasant to touch, not at all frightening, as I expected, and so alive. This is in direct contrast to my previous experience of him as cold, sharp, critical, tough, nail-like bristly bearded, rough and crude.

Inside my mother's chest, I reach for the tiny almond heart and hold it between forefinger and thumb. To my utter amazement, the almond is pulsing in a slow, gentle, regular beat between my fingers. Tears well up in my eyes. Dick uses this opportunity to move me to another image— one of myself as a two-week-old infant nursing at my mother's breast. The warm, sweet milk flows into my mouth abundantly and easily, filling my body with a sense of well-being and love. I remain here, taking in all I can hold until I am full.

I am aware of a couple of major changes my mother passed through that affected me profoundly as an infant, child, and young man, that I am aware of now, although I do not know what in her own life precipitated these. She was in her prime in my infancy and this seems to be the phase of parenting that enthralled her, from which she derived the greatest satisfaction. As I grew into childhood, however, she became increasingly cautious, fearful, and conservative. By the time she started through menopause I was a young man, but I remember it as a rough time for her. In my mind this is when the image of her as small, tight, and afraid solidified.

At this point in my journey, Dick urges me to move forward in time to about the age of eight years old and asks me to call up the image of our living room, which was off limits to us as children. The sofa is white, the carpets are white, the walls are white. The wall at the far end is lined with mirrored shelves with crystal figurines displayed on them. The sofa is covered in clear plastic, and the whiteness everywhere is not unlike the diamond cave in my previous journey. Dick suggests that I make myself comfortable in the living room. He has my mother come in and sit quietly on the sofa with me.

Now my father arrives and gets down on his hands and knees so that he is close to my height. Playfully he invites me to wrestle with him, which we never did before. As we get into it, he knows just how to challenge me to the level that my eight-year-old body can handle. I fight him back with all my might and knock him over and roll on top of him, exerting my force to bring him into submission. Then he strives with all his might to overcome my power and, lo and behold, we roll over in the other direction so that he is now on top and in charge and I am momentarily defeated. And so we go, back and forth, alternately tasting of victory and defeat, fully engaged in each other. Now my father on his knees rears up on his haunches and bows down low to me. As he comes up from the bow, I see that he is the Buddha. In my delight I bow to him also, and this gesture completes the journey.

If we choose to call up our memories, stretch ourselves to pull from past experience, we can benefit from the many layers and levels of events. When we keep the memory alive by turning its soil, we have an enormous amount of material to bring with us to every meeting with another. Most of us choose to have our experience on the surface and then bury it deep below. Whatever is planted doesn't break through from below because it's planted too deep. We forget it. In journeying anew into old territory, first we call up the history as we knew it. Then we call up a different story, but one that is also clearly ours, allowing us to view the old and the new side by side. Henceforth we carry these two visions with us. We know the emptiness, loss, or hardness endured with the first. We also know the warmth and softness of the new encounter. From this point on, we have a broader, fertile, better cultivated soil from which to grow all our relationships.

On this journey with Dick I have been nurtured and guided in ways I wasn't as a boy. These vivid eidetic images allow me to experience a new reality. The human mind is magical in this respect. Once an event is in the past, the mind does not have to distinguish between what happened in "real" life versus the imaging work. Both impact us as if we were there. The images brought to life in this journey are strong enough for me to keep and draw upon as needed. When I finish the journey I feel a tremendous sense of relief. I feel balanced—poised for the present, ready for the future. Being there for the ones we love and for others in our community—what we call service—is inspiring. Each of us needs to find ways—big and small, depending on our stage of life—to step up into this arena.

You can take your own journey. Find a place that comforts you. See it. Breathe it in. Enter the picture and let the scene evolve. Find yourself before a spirit guide, one that welcomes you and with great caring shares some truths with you. Thank that guide and return to the awake present with focused and renewed energy. Our life's work is an ever-evolving story. At any point we can re-direct our energies and go from holding in, holding down, or holding back to coming forth and giving to others. Our lives can be about affirming life and the generosity that stirs within. ◆

Man in Service

All too often, men don't go the distance and obtain for themselves what they need to lead a healthy life. This makes us feel cheated. In this victimized condition, we tend not to give back to our communities what we gain from them and what they need from us. The same is true for our families. When we feel put upon by them, used up by them, we withhold what they need to become strong. The remaining portion of this chapter is devoted to a discussion of these issues. What we're looking for is a new emotional and psychological perspective.

If we can free ourselves from the shortcomings of our individual histories, it allows us to be available in intimate relationships and in service to the world in which we live. As you understand your own development and the crucial experiences that have shaped your adulthood, be aware of the parts that still interfere with your availability to do what you need to do. When we accept these limitations, face them honestly, bring into our lives whatever might be missing, then are we free to set sail.

In a crisis it is typical for men to act. Usually it is for the benefit of others, often on behalf of those weaker or less able, and sometimes in disregard of their own well-being and safety. We go to war for our country, serve corporations at the expense of our sanity, gather the injured in times of disaster, run into burning buildings, dive into dark and freezing waters to save the drowning, and so on. It's a tradition. On the other hand, men often ignore signals that are less than crisis in nature or proportion.

The things we ignore are those which require daily nurturance, such as nourishing a relationship, caring for a young child, or nurturing an employee who needs special attention. When human energy is required for these endeavors, men tend to take a back seat and see to their own needs. When men come to accept responsibility toward others in this realm (normal daily life) as well as to themselves, whole new avenues open up for them to enrich their personal lives.

Most men and now women are taught that the major route to happiness is through individual achievement in some field of work. In reality the activities that enhance our sense of well-being, build depth of character and keep us in good health are fathering, husbanding, and mentoring others—with the goal of making the world and our communities better places to live. By fathering we mean taking responsibility for the general well-being of those people who are in our lives.

In our own weekend workshops, some men who have been through the Men's Room program return to be "service men." In this capacity, they serve as part of a team of men who are already working on developing relationships with each other. Their responsibility as service men is to observe, notice, support, serve, and father the other participants in the weekend. This may be anything from comforting someone in emotional distress, to taking a walk to pursue a discussion started in a group session, to helping provide for a range of physical needs. Service men are responsible for building a context of safety and trust so that others feel secure enough to speak from the depth of their hearts about the real issues that concern them. But the reward for the service men stretches way beyond any one weekend of giving. And this is the point. The soul itself expands when one reaches out to help, especially when one helps another begin the process of bringing himself into community and genuine contact with other men.

The Old Way is Dead

Most men learn the following code of conduct: "I will be responsible for myself, I will be independent, and I will diligently, vigilantly protect the one ego that makes all this possible for me—my own." This orientation results in a narcissistic cycle of self-involvement. Over generations it causes intense difficulty in relationships between men and their partners as well as in other relationships. When a man can balance the process of looking after himself and tending to the needs of others on a daily basis, he experiences a deep level of fulfillment and satisfaction.

During the Men's Room weekend it is wonderful to witness the transition between the Friday evening arrival and

Sunday's conclusion. On Friday the new men know next to nothing of what is to come. Most of them don't know anyone else in the group. Although they sit next to one another, you can see the calculated isolation in which each holds himself. As the weekend progresses, this distance closes for most of the men present. A tone is set as feelings are discovered and disclosed and then one by one the men will risk reaching out to one another. Contact from the heart begins, either with words spoken or through eye contact, and usually evolves into a supportive hand on the shoulder or embrace. At this point the transformation of primary focus, from self to other, occurs.

For many men this represents the first time they are in authentic contact with another person outside of marriage, love partnership, or early childhood contact with parents. This quality and depth of contact cannot take place unless we are willing to face an important part of our identity: the need for acceptance, recognition, and love. It requires us as well to face our own envy, jealousy, self-doubt, and self-importance. We have to drop some of the normal barriers and, especially, we need to move beyond our preoccupation with doing only what men are *supposed* to do. If we act out of obligation or insincerity we have missed the opportunity. To do this work effectively, to grow from it, it has to come from the heart.

All men possess a generosity of spirit, a natural propensity to give. Yet because so many of us have been trained to focus on ourselves and the image we're trying to project, we find the giving posture awkward at first. Our hope is that as you read on, you will also begin the process of uncovering, of digging down below the surface to locate your own generosity of spirit. This is where you will find the clear motivation to love, to nurture, support and applaud others. The more you use it the stronger it grows.

Heart Paths

Recently a Men's Room participant who has also remained active in his post-weekend "keep it up" group had a wedding. It was a second marriage and he invited an array of friends, old and new. The men who attended from The Men's Room stood out in the crowd, not only because of their spirited and warm camaraderie (it was a kind of reunion for these men as well as a wedding) but also because of the way they conducted themselves. Each of them, for example, brought the bride and groom a gift, and it was clear from the way the gift was presented (however small it might be) that a great deal of care was involved. Other friends chose the traditional route of sending a gift separately.

In a chance meeting a couple of months later, the groom chuckled about the number of gifts promised which hadn't yet arrived from several old friends . . . who were duly chagrined, as they provided apologies and bemoaned the lack of time available to fulfill the promise. The groom was not complaining. Like most of us he well understands the time constraints of the day. He noted, however, the distinct approach to giving among his Men's Room friends. There was a clear sense conveyed of: "This person matters to me, and it is important for me to do what I need to do, to let him know he and his new wife are cared for." These men make a commitment to honor each other's life processes, goals, important events, and families. The giving of gifts in this context is an important symbol of that commitment and it goes beyond the usual sense of isolated obligation.

Our perceptions of what we can do to make life better for ourselves and others involves a willingness to relinquish, to sacrifice. This is not an easy shift for most men to make. We encourage each other to face this discomfort up front. A new perspective and commitment are required to make it work for us. This takes time, a certain amount of self-discovery and self-acceptance. Eventually men learn that in engaging our spirit of generosity we actually decrease our dependency on others because we don't expect them to do our giving or our living for us.

Among Children

Perhaps you noticed that while we're writing this book, we're moving from one location to another. Each place is selected for a reason. Sometimes we know the reason, sometimes we don't. For the chapter on fathers we chose the cemetery where Buddy's father and uncle are buried. Other times, like today, we pick a place and let the reason make itself known. For the wrap-up of this chapter, we're at Gillison Park just north of Chicago on the lake in Wilmette, Illinois.

Ancient trees of lush plumage are rooted in rolling, gardened hills spooned up to a wide ribbon of sand that spans several miles of lake front. The bluest sky holds low-slung puff-white clouds that move in tandem with the blue gray chop of Lake Michigan shimmering in the distance. We have settled in at the edge of a large outdoor amphitheater. A few minutes ago a group of instructors briefed a gathering of several hundred young children in preparation for a trip to the waterfront. Right now the children, in a splendid array of color, ages, sizes, and shapes—boys and girls laughing and talking—swirl by us in slow motion like a rainbowed river flowing out to sea.

Here is a moving portrait of generosity of spirit. We take them in, a blessed vision, not a mob running wild, helter skelter. They come in groups of two, three, four or more, arm in arm, hand over shoulder, hand in hand talking and walking toward their next event. These children have been parented and coached from one event to the next. It is as it should be and could be, we observe. But who among us will bring this to pass? Who will take the journey with the children from the towns of Could Be and Should Be to those of Always and Will Be generous of spirit?

When we were young and among the children, we depended entirely on the generosity of spirit of the adults around us. Without it we could not survive. In towns and cities across the land and around the globe, the ability of the adults to provide the crucial ingredients of time and concerned guidance is crippled and dwindling. Even in our wealthiest communities, the children are raising themselves, often on a diet of low-grade TV, fashion trends, and early sexual experience, raising themselves to the beat of grunge amidst imminent violence, fatal disease, death by overdose— practicing by default a do-it-yourself adulthood for Life according to MTV and Hollywood. We know that the children who receive no generosity of spirit cannot give it either. We know as well that these children are having children of their own, as we speak. Placing this dark note next to the bright vision of possibility, a river of children well cared for, we know it is time to commit ourselves anew to a generosity of spirit that can seize today and lead the way.

The Road Out

When some of us start to examine our lives, we automatically note how we messed up, what we ought to be doing but aren't. We feel guilty, shameful, or resentful. These feelings can siphon off the energy required for us to begin giving. The purpose of self-examination is to encourage us to push on the boundaries, to expand our lives toward greater reward.

When you find yourself feeling guilty, turn it into a stepping stone instead. As Dick Olney puts it, "That life is over so this one can begin."

The road to hell, as the axiom goes, is paved with good intentions. We remind ourselves now that the road out of hell is paved with the same thing. Intentions are motivators, tools for learning to become our own guides and leaders. They help us follow through on action plans in a timely, authentic manner. We make an intention now to take a new step each day in bringing ourselves into service in the world. Men have an immense job ahead, a major role to play in fathering their own children and the children of the communities in which they live. Here is an opportunity for each of us to provide much-needed guidance and hope for the next generation.

SEVEN

Man in Relationship

Stress in our lives at home, work, and in the world at large can be processed, balanced, and ultimately alleviated by choosing to utilize the healing properties of significant relationships with other people. Intimate relationships— whether between friends or spouses, or with children or the elderly in our lives, are essential to our health. We need to be in relationship in order to feel whole.

■ **At birth** and for a time thereafter most of us experience the most perfect relationship we will ever know. It matters not who or what we are or where we came from. Only *that* we are. Even when the biological mother is unable, others come forward to feed and adore. In the death camps of Nazi Germany, there were instances when starving male prisoners lactated, produced milk in their breasts in response to the cries of motherless newborns. Hearts open, milk flows like love, and Mother Nature herself may bend over backwards to make this connection work.

Never again will we receive or be given to in this manner—without reservation, utterly vulnerable, naked, swaddled in love. There is a fall from grace in all that follows as paradise recedes. There's the relentless march of conditions to be met, the layer upon layer of our identity accumulating—composed of who we are, who we appear to be, and the parts of us we must hide in order to survive the climb to adulthood, the natural course of growing up. Generally we emerge partly civilized. Partly we remain hidden and frequently we are distressed to one degree or another. In merely surviving we are changed forever and left with a profound sense of loss. Intact, however, is the memory of paradise and a longing to recapture the wholeness, the health, and the glory of this first awakening in relationship. Men often tell us of their desire to have women just *know* them, without struggle, without complication. It sounds so like an early developmental stage. It is.

In all subsequent intimate relationships we strive on some level to replicate our experience in the first one. The problem for most of us is that these strivings remain unconscious, unacknowledged, and somewhat unrealistic. So the intimate relationships in which we find ourselves continue to mystify and plague us for their shortcomings.

In each initial Men's Room weekend, we introduce the notion of creating conscious intimate relationships that are intended from the start to fill a universal human need to be connected, known, recognized, and accepted for who we are. These relationships can provide us with the nourishment and support each of us needs to become more of who we want to be. It isn't exactly the same as that first love of infancy. On our own, however, we don't stand a chance. Men need to see that intimacy and depth of contact are not the preserve of women only. They need to experience the potential for accomplishing for themselves as adults something close to what was intended for the child—the quality of contact and nourishment needed for health and survival.

Profound Everyday Discoveries

BUDDY ▼ Our first chapter described the birth of our own relationship, of Buddy and Bob back in 1982. You recall that I was initially enamored of Bob's intellect. "I want your brain," is how I put it when we were paired together in an exercise on intimacy. Over the following months and years, as our friendship developed a rich topsoil of trust, we were able to go deeper, to penetrate the roots of our feelings and beliefs. For example, when I peel back the layer of my desire that I label "intellect," I discover what I really want is to be recognized and respected. Peeling back yet another layer, I can simply say: "I need love." The deeper we go the more we discover how much we have in common with others. One man's issue is every man's issue. ▼

BOB ◆ We do not need to be loved for who we *seem* to be but rather for *who we are.* My first statement to Buddy in that exercise on intimacy long ago was, "I want your hair," for the obvious reason that I am balding. This was a difficult disclosure for me to make—an admission of vanity, having the thought that the hair makes the man. But the real cause of my discomfort remained hidden until I knew and trusted Buddy much better. It was months before I could explain to him how I experienced my first and major hair loss years before when I was attempting to stay out of the Vietnam War.

It was a time of great pain and turmoil for me. Over a period of many months I was torn up by two conflicting emotions: fear of dying and shame at avoiding the call to serve. Not surprisingly, my body registered the conflict in spades. My hair fell out. It happened rapidly, almost overnight . . . in gobs. There is no doubt in my mind that the

hair loss represented in part a question regarding my in-
nermost sense of myself. Am I the man I claim to be? And
who would that be? Beneath the words, "I want your hair"
is the story of a young man's coming to terms, as all
men must, with the values that inform our actions and
determine the direction lives will take. I avoided the draft
all right, but it cost me my hair and provided me a permanent reminder of my *sin*—an infraction of my own
ideals. ◆

Only when we strip back the masks, the shields of pre-
tense, and get real with one another, can the tattered and
torn in us emerge. The wounds, the parts we instinctively
hide, are what most want knowing. When we trust enough
to let another into the inner sanctum, to give him or her a
view of the whole of us rather than the pretty picture we dis-
play by light of day, we open the door to possibility and
growth. This is the place where genuine intimacy, reciprocity, and healing can begin.

The reason we hesitate is because it is also the place where
we can encounter the greatest pain, for the arena of *relationship* is the cradle of our discontent as well as the birthplace of
our happiness and health. We can use the agony of loss or
rejection in our relationships as an excuse never to become
vulnerable again, or as fuel to propel us forward. No relationship is fail safe. But if we choose to establish and build relationships designed for distance, depth, and support we stand
to gain from the pain.

Neither suffering nor joy is a necessary product of vulnerability. But chances are a full life will know both. And the
only way to live fully is to open up. The process of self-disclosure, of revealing the heart of darkness, the fear and vulnerability as well as our light, is not a decision we can make once
and for all. It is, rather, a choice we make for ourselves every
day. Getting good at it takes practice.

Four Stages of Conscious Intimacy

In our work with men we divide the development of a conscious intimate relationship into four stages. Think of them in terms of mountain climbing. Imagine yourself and a friend leaving your car in a parking lot at a mountain wilderness park. Much of your security—cellular phone, luggage, things of comfort—is locked up and left behind. You embark on the initial part of the hike. Drawn toward the mountain, the breathtaking views, you stride confidently along well-worn trails and flat land. Conversation is about what is before you. It is light and easy. Stage One, *Embarking,* entails the easy ground-breaking conversations that lead to a decision to create a new connection with a significant person in our lives.

Once we reach the base of the mountain the incline grows steadily upward. The path is no longer smooth and straight. We have alternative paths to choose among. We wander some, we negotiate around steeper sections. Our pace is affected by that of our climbing partner. We discuss it. We intuit it. We encourage each other. Mostly, though, we discover the ways in which we can depend on each other. Stage Two, *Exploration,* invites us to maneuver, test, and stretch our abilities relative to another. It begins with disclosure of our whole selves, including our darker aspects, and works its way into welcoming and challenging others along similar paths.

Now the ascent begins in earnest. On the mountain, all our muscles are in use as we pull ourselves upward with our arms, extend our legs fully to reach a toehold, or jump from one rock to another, calling on back, stomach, and other muscles to balance ourselves. We climb along ledges narrow enough to raise questions in our minds about flying and falling, stopping occasionally to catch our breath. We find it's best to do this close to a climbing partner so he can give a hand, steady you, call out encouragement. Stage Three, *Ascension,* is where we exert ourselves, push ourselves to make history with our partner, sharing deep and essential parts of our lives so that we are now experiencing some mutual joy or sorrow in each other's victories and defeats.

Cresting toward the top of the mountain we are exhilarated by the sense of accomplishment. Together we have experienced meeting a challenge. We have done this both independently and as a partnership. We share the physical exertion, the mental concentration, the emotional fears, frustrations, and exhilarations, and the spiritual renewal that comes from being one with another and at peace with the world. Stage Four, *Emergence,* is experienced when the relationship reaches an acknowledged and celebrated spiritual plane. There are peak experiences of sharing that may have aspects that are beyond words. Yet, in having emerged through them together, our bond is strengthened and helps us to confidently approach the next ascent.

These four stages pertain to an intimate relationship with anyone—of the same or opposite sex, be they friends, lovers, or family members. The presence or absence of sexual involvement is actually irrelevant. A sexual relationship can exist with little or no intimate contact between partners. Intimacy has to do with emotional closeness. Our society tends to define sex as a form of intimacy, which it can be but isn't necessarily. Rape, for example, is the antithesis of intimacy.

STAGE ONE: *Embarking*

The first stage of relationship building involves the willingness to come out of isolation and to begin making contact with another. In this case, the connection is made with the intention of pursuing more than a superficial relationship. This is not about getting together to talk about sports, business, and politics—a gruesome threesome when used, as they often are, to avoid intimacy. This is about making a conscious choice to come out of seclusion and make authentic contact with another human being, in this case, another man. This is the stage that the two of us entered when we first agreed to meet for breakfast Friday mornings. We were ready to sit down together and say to one another, "Tell me more." In Stage One we focus on building a level of trust that will accommodate the growth of intimacy.

The men on our weekends embark on their relationships after the weekend is over. They can join a leaderless group that meets every two or three weeks. Men tell us how difficult it is to maintain the kind of openness, honesty, and energy that they had experienced during the weekend. They struggle to find a cohesive way to continue their dialogue without reverting to guy-talk. We get called. "How do we do this?" "What topics should we discuss?" We focus them on what's in the room—the group, the struggle, the feelings that are with them in the moment.

Roger told us that his group would "check in with each other about meaningful events in our lives. Then we provide a safe haven for one of the guys to talk about something that's difficult for him. We look out for each other. We don't solve things. Slowly, we're beginning to take emotional risks, revealing ourselves. The first strands of a web are being strung."

Frequency and continuity of contact are essential in building relationship. This means picking up the telephone, making a call, not just to schedule handball or exercise or lunch. You pick up the phone to let the other person know you're thinking of him, that you remember what is going on in his life. You have a stake in the outcome of the other's special events, and you want to keep the other informed about yours. There has to be a mutual commitment to keep the flow going. Continuity requires that you recall and honor what has gone on in your previous contact. This builds the mutual history and deepens the opportunity for exploration. The memorable moments of male bonding go beyond the fishing trip or sailing holiday, beyond the beating of drums or building a house together. Their roots are also in the mood and nuance of our daily lives.

STAGE TWO: *Exploration*

In Stage Two both partners allow themselves to become more *vulnerable* and more *volatile* in the relationship. Between us this includes acknowledging our weaknesses and deficiencies as well as spelling out a shift we intend to make in our lives. Each of us settles on a shift that will benefit every relationship we are involved in.

Stage Two presumes that a level of trust has already been established. We were not ready for Stage Two until we developed a friendship of several months. Both of us had to reach a point where we felt the other would be willing to support the intended shift and provide honest feedback as the work progressed.

There will be times when you begin to form a relationship with someone which you hope will grow, but it doesn't. Getting oneself ready is part of the equation. The other part is finding a willing and capable partner with whom to work. This can be difficult because men habitually hold themselves to superficial contact, an easy connection that guards against any penetration into territory where vulnerabilities show.

BOB ◆ A major shift I set out to manage was about my tendency to soften the presentation of my opinions. I developed this style in response to my father whose presentation was always overcharged, often angry, and rarely tempered by considerations of impact. Where my father was emotional, loud-mouthed, and offensive, I became soft-spoken, objective, and compulsively inoffensive to the point where it held me back from being candid, assertive, and comfortable handling criticism from others. By the same token when I wanted to question the actions of others, I carefully qualified every comment. I was too hesitant and self-conscious. For example, I might say, "I really don't mean to upset you, and I don't want you to take this too strongly, because I don't mean it in the way that you might think. If it upsets you we can talk about it . . . but a little bit of the time you have a tendency to be too gruff with me."

The shift I wanted to make was to begin communicating in a straightforward manner without sweeteners, minus the adjectives. I was determined to practice direct delivery of my ideas and to allow my emotions freer play. Here's the direct version: *"You're fairly gruff with me."*

The result is simple enough, but the road taken was not at all. ◆

BUDDY ▼ The big shift for me came later, in the middle of one of our early experiential weekends, which at that point were still held in the city of Evanston. During the lunch break, Bob and I walked to a nearby park to exchange thoughts on how the weekend was going. We agreed it was on target.

Then, quite unexpectedly, Bob turned to me and said, "You know, Buddy, you are good at what you do. These men are impressed with your ability to deal with the issues that are foremost in their lives; they are impressed with your command of your own life. You are gifted in your ability to articulate other's concerns and your timing is excellent. But I'm starting to notice something else too. There is a bit of 'neonness,' a certain flashiness to your presentation, as if you have it *all* together. So what I want to ask you is, Where are the other parts? Where is your pain? Where is your sadness? I'm blinded by the light. I, for one, need to experience you on a deeper level."

I was astonished. I knew exactly what he was talking about. My heart began to pound. He was on to my *"shine."* I felt exposed and embarrassed. And then, because it was Bob, I felt relief. Out at last and in safe company.

As a child, my family needed me to shine. Both my parents labeled me as special from the beginning. My mother expected me to be strong and independent. My father was a warm, gentle spirit, but passive. Even though I had an older brother, I was considered the special one, strong enough to take care of the family—charming, verbal, and engaging. Also, I was physically able, a natural athlete. In school I quickly became the center of attention, even though I did poorly academically. Academically, I was lost. Everything up to it had been so easy for me, but the school work—I couldn't hack it. So I just ignored that part, pretended it didn't exist.

"If only Buddy would apply himself," became the nagging refrain of teachers and parents alike. To the other kids, however, I was the coolest, the most outspoken— funny and fearless. If ever there was a fight brewing, I jumped into it. I thrived on the attention.

In retrospect I think I used this edge, this *shine*, to cover up what was for me a shameful learning disability that continued to torment me well into adulthood. The fact of the matter was . . . I could not read. When I finally learned to read, the words formed slowly, as if coming to me through a fog. It used to take me hours to complete assignments that others did in minutes. Yet no one suspected. I was verbally quick, and in the realm of emotions and relationships I was ahead of my years, more mature, completely dependable. Thus I kept my secret intact for years.

When Bob confronted me, I had to accept it. I had heard this about myself before—my one-man-show, Mr. Finesse. What I didn't realize was the cost. While my *shine* was gaining me recognition and approval I craved, it called my credibility into question. People were wonder-

ing if that's all there is—a strutting, self-assured, enter-
taining guy. If that's all there is, how authentic can this
guy be? They were aware they were seeing a part of me,
and not beyond.

In pursuing my shift I did not give up the shine. Instead
I began to let my insecurities show—my fears, anxieties,
and concerns. These new aspects added dimension and
lessened the focus on my shining side. As people's expectations of me relaxed, so did I. My efforts were rewarded.
Those close to me began to comment on how good it was
for them to see this kind of human struggle. They could
identify with me. This gave me the courage to persist in
the shift, to continue sharing my less developed parts
more openly with people. ▼

The shifts we elect to make involve ingrained behavior
developed over a lifetime, behavior that will always be
present to some extent; it is part of us. Each of us needs to be
alert to the part of us that would show only what looks good.
We need to become conscious of the instinct to run for cover,
to hide our vulnerability. When we learn to notice how we
are, we can then search for key behavior to add in order to
move into balance. The hardest part of making a shift is
coming to terms with one's deficiencies, owning the issues
involved, understanding their rightful place in our past development, and acknowledging our need to move on. The
exciting part is in opening to the possibilities and seeing that
there is a safe place to begin this kind of work.

It is doubtful that these kinds of shifts can be made without someone on the outside providing feedback. In our relationship we had to learn to be clear, direct, and actively supportive, to take the time to make the relationship itself
strong enough to incubate the work that each of us set out to
accomplish. It requires commitment and a willingness to
greet frustration and backpedaling as necessary to progress.

One of the hardest parts we encountered was our mutual fear of disturbing the developing intimacy by injecting honest feedback. We held back a lot, we avoided the risk involved, we avoided talking about what we were avoiding. But gradually one learns to trust, especially as the shifts we make in the relationship come alive, as they propel us forward into deeper experiences with each other.

Self-examination and self-discovery are key players. This means dropping our normal defenses, hearing what we don't want to hear about things we do that we know about, but keep buried because to look at them is unpleasant. Often we spot our own undesirable qualities in others before we are able to look at them in ourselves. One of the best ways of getting past defenses is to acknowledge their usefulness, honor their positive contribution. Our defenses serve to keep us on track. They screen out "superfluous" information, all the things going on around us that distract us from our essential path of the moment. But like the guard dog who knows only one master, they stave off the good news as well as the bad. Whatever rides in is fair game. As often as they protect us from unnecessary distraction, they also shield us from the truth and from dealing with situations we need to confront. With this understanding of our defenses, we can learn to recognize and then relax them on occasion.

The perceptions of others can help us penetrate our defenses. Ask a trusted friend, spouse, or partner, "What do you see in me? Tell me about the good and not so good." Notice we do not ask this question often. Mostly we would rather not know. When we are ready for it, however, a great deal of information is available.

It isn't that other people really know us better than we know ourselves. It's that others don't have a stake in looking the other way. They have their own set of defenses to worry about. Like you and me, they are more apt to spot someone else's shortcomings than their own. Not everything we hear about ourselves is true. But when we are ready to listen, we usually know it when the truth comes marching in, whether the news is good or not.

No matter how well we manage to hide the things about ourselves that we find less than ideal, they are real. They persist. And one way or the other they find expression in our lives. If we want to manage that expression, direct it, balance it, we need to know about it. Most of all we need to discover that we are not loved in *spite of our flaws,* but *in addition to* them.

For the men who continue beyond the weekend, exploration means sticking in there with each other. Feelings may get bruised, trust damaged, as each man tries out new behaviors of honesty, caring confrontation, or self-disclosure. After six years in a group, one of the men wrote: "I have had some self-loathing, and shame about aspects of myself come up. I am judgmental, never good enough, and jealous. For a long time I denied all this—to my wife, colleagues, and Men's Room friends. The group has helped show these to me in non-shaming ways. They've helped me see that I can't hide it or shove it away. It will never go away. I'm beginning to accept it in me as they do and with that I can see myself catching it sometimes, poking fun at myself about it. As I learn to live with it, with their help, I'm a better friend to them and the other important people in my life."

Our first group of men continues to meet a decade later. By the end of their first year they began a tradition other groups have followed. They threw a dinner party to celebrate their bond. Intimate others came. The men had done all the planning and preparations. They greeted each other at the door with hugs and introductions of their spouses or companions. They gathered in the kitchen to cook with animated conversation and eagerness to share with each other. It was natural. Meanwhile, a reversal of roles was happening. Despite conversations at home about who would be there and introductions at the event, the women were confronted with the stilted tension of talking with others they had not met, weren't sure if they'd be with again or have anything in common with. They felt the estrangement, a sense of out-of-touch-ness that is so common to men under the reversed circumstances.

STAGE THREE: *Ascension*

> **BOB** ◆ In the third stage the relationship takes on a life of its own. There is no rushing into Stage Three. It can only occur after considerable time has been spent together. In this stage the line between us begins to take on a translucent and fluid aspect. There are pivotal moments of being there for each other, willing to join in celebration or enter the other's sadness or fear. For example, when our relationship entered the third stage, it meant experiencing together the possibility of losing our parents. It involved facing the substance abuse problem of Buddy's stepson and the *angst* I experienced over the departure of my daughters for college. ◆

> **BUDDY** ▼ When my stepson became addicted to cocaine, Bob walked right through the experience with me. Not only did he counsel my stepson directly, but he helped my wife and me through the anguish of our own distrust. Because he could be more objective, Bob showed us our son's need for independence if he was to be successful in recovery. He helped us see what questions we needed answers to and which ones we did not, how to communicate with him in ways that were respectful of the battle he was fighting and the integrity he was trying to restore. We were very lucky, of course, to have a friend who also has considerable experience in treating addictions. But regardless of his professional expertise, our relationship was such that he considered our plight his own. This

quality of involvement played a pivotal role in my stepson's progress. ▼

For the groups that continue, as most do, this stage brings them face-to-face with encouraging and leaning on others to continue to grow, evolve. The men try out other workshops, conferences. They engage in new activities with their wives. They bring this into the group and progress into more direct, honest, non-shaming sharing.

At the same time, life has a way of presenting material that causes each of them to struggle up the ascent. Parents passing away, children dating or marrying, divorces, re-connections to spouses, moves, job loss—the list is long and not surprising. It is life's list. But in the group, with friends who climb with you, each new challenge is seen, examined, dealt with honestly and helps the next man engage with the next event more meaningfully.

Stuart told us: "I've dropped some of my earlier friends. I just couldn't get the same feeling with them. With my new friends I know it's okay to admit, to say I'm scared or I don't know. I learned that a man can be scared and still be a man. I learned that it's okay to not always be in control and that when I lose control of a situation I can still keep my dignity. I know that there is strength in vulnerability. That was once an oxymoron, now it's a truth that guides me."

STAGE FOUR: *Emergence*

Stage Four of a conscious intimate relationship is when the partners emerge onto a spiritual journey together. We do not mean a religious journey, although a religious journey might be part of a spiritual quest. By spiritual we mean *of spirit,* a realm of experience that transcends the here and now.

There is certainly a spiritual component to all relationships. However brief or fleeting, spirits trade fare when two people make contact. An imprint of a kind that cannot be seen, measured, or put wholly into words is made, one upon another. A brief mingling of mental/emotional energy takes place and stays with us when we part. In casual or superficial encounters we generally rein in the spirit. Normal boundaries between spirits tend to dissolve only under events of a dramatic nature. They also come down naturally as an intimate relationship evolves through the first three stages.

Stage Four presumes an attitude of openness toward the unknown, an inclination to search for meaning beyond material and physical reality, a willingness to move into other spheres of knowing and existence. It assumes the possibility of spiritual unity between two people and between us and the universe outside ourselves. It may well provide the basis for a greater level of intimacy between partners than can be experienced in previous stages.

The spiritual stage in intimate relationship can begin in a formal manner, such as deciding to meditate together or getting involved in one of any number of spiritual practices (yoga, *Tai Chi*, etc.) or disciplines (playing music together, running, gardening, community service, etc.). Or, it can take place informally as the two or more partners devise private rituals and make room in their everyday lives for honoring and attending to the spiritual realm. Two men we know take a silent walk together once a week to renew their spirit, honor their connection to nature, their origins in nature, and their desire to strengthen the environment. At the end of the walk, they sit and share thoughts, feelings, or plans that arise out of their contemplation.

Another route into the spiritual realm can open up when we simply stumble into another reality, one which escaped our awareness in the past. Usually, though, there is a precipitating factor—an illness, a loss, a sudden and profound change in circumstances. These are the incubators of the spiritual quest. When we come up against our own limitations and those of the material world, we begin to look beyond them for sustenance.

Over and over again we hear men speak of the love they have found in their friendships. They speak with an awe that captures us and them. Corwin wrote: "I found a friend. In fact, my best friend. Doesn't that have a wonderful feeling to it? Best friend. What a wish-fulfilling, heart-ringing thing this is to me. The smile on my face goes clear to my heart." Another said: "Deep connections with others fill my life, fill the hole that would otherwise be there. I have acquired a web of friends through this work who speak a common language of truth, who have and will take emotional risks with each other. We are each other's safe haven in a world filled with challenge. The deeper I go with them the more I feel love for and from my wife and children."

Man's Hunger for Man

One of the strongest elements of our weekend experiences with men is for them to see the kind of relationship that the two of us have. It is important for us to make clear that ours has many imperfections and is still emerging. But we are two men who love one another, who have developed a powerful bond in a non-sexual relationship. We do not intend to red-flag the non-sexual aspect, although it is important. Gay men have the same needs as heterosexual men for connection with other men in a safe, respectful relationship that includes a sense of brotherhood and deep compassion for the welfare of the other person.

Stress in our lives at home, work, and in the world at large can be processed, balanced, and ultimately alleviated by choosing to utilize the healing properties of significant relationships with other people. Intimate relationships are essential to our health. We need to be in relationship in order to feel whole.

Because of profound changes in what is expected of men in our society, many of us have articulated a need for new traditions of bonding. One of these is to be involved in a small number of close friendships with other men. Without these we end up feeling alone and frequently depressed. In our isolation we continue to question the meaning of our existence. Or, we find refuge among women with whom we sometimes feel freer to connect, free to not compete, able to express our emotions without feeling foolish. If we restrict our close relationships to women, however, we short-change our own gender and ourselves in the process. When men single out women for direction, balance, and emotional support that we are not willing to provide for each other, we deny ourselves access to a major source of growth and sense of well-being.

By Saturday night on the weekend, a community of friends has begun. The unsteady men of Friday night have become the honest, honorable, grounded men of Saturday night. Ascension, connection is in progress. As with much of life what goes up must come down. There is ebb and flow, *yin* and *yang*, soft and hard, dark and light. With well-being in their hearts the men sleep soundly. Sunday morning begins with imagery that takes them deeply into the shadowy crevices where they've hidden shameful parts of themselves. Hiding these parts has compressed, restricted their spirit. As you turn to the next chapter, prepare yourself to enter a visual journey and the thoughts of men as they go into a deeper, darker land, to expand and enliven themselves.

EIGHT

Journey into the
Dark Self

■ **A slice of sand** pierces the dark glass of the lake where thirty men gather at dawn beneath the gnarled yellow branches of an ancient black willow tree. Rooted in the dark the men stretch and warm up to the movement of *Tai Chi*. When the sun peaks the horizon light shimmers across the water and the stage comes to life. It looks like the men are limbs of the tree and the beach itself is breathing.

Hugh

He takes us overland across days of scrub growth and desert. Nary a tree breaks the monotony so we are nearly grateful when, exhausted, we butt up against a sheer wall rising straight up from the canyon floor. No way around in either direction and as we look up, the top is out of sight as well, or seems to be. Turning ninety degrees northward we proceed in single file. Our left shoulders catch the morning heat that pours off the rock between the shiny black shadows. Behind us, to the east, the sun blisters our backsides on its slow climb upward. Dripping with sweat, we are dying to stop, but the beat of the drum drives us on . . .

Ahhh, my neck is cramping up. Am I taking this too seriously? Just a little trip. No big deal. No clue what the others are thinking . . . When I just let go I slip right into step. If anybody would have told me about this yesterday, I would've laughed out loud. Now it's not so funny.

At noon we are spared momentarily as each man's shadow slides to the floor and attaches to the one in front of it so the path is shaded for a time. Men come here to heal injuries, fractures in their lives—hairline or marrow deep. Soon enough the time comes for us to enter our shame, excavate the dirt, relinquish our secrets. No time to rest, though, as Buddy's voice urges us forward, echoing down the line, like a magnet pulling us along.

Aarron

As the last man I imagine five or ten others in front of me, sometimes twenty out of the thirty as we spread out and snake northward. At odd intervals there are notches scooped out of the rock, like upright craters, some as wide as twenty paces, before the wall juts eastward and resumes the northern route. Thus before me my dirty companions disappear and reappear as if snatched up and regurgitated moments later by some unseen but playful creature who isn't that hungry. Dusk comes and the canyon's own shadow subsumes all others, the edge of it racing eastward to meet the cold night air.

To my astonishment each man does disappear now, one by one. Front to back, the line of men is snipped shorter and shorter until alone I reach what looks to be the edge of another notch. Turning the corner I find myself staring into an aperture the size of a two-story house, pitch black, save for the gaping lip of it sucking in the last pink rays of the setting sun. Out of the blackness come the moans of my companions as Buddy's voice leads the entire party inward and down toward what inner sanctum none of us knows yet. The breakfast I ate so long ago threatens to unseat itself.

I plunge into the darkness to catch up, as Buddy's voice is calling out, "Try to keep together or you'll get lost. Here is the dungeon. Inside there are stairs. Watch your step, keep one hand on the shoulder of the man in front of you. At the bottom there are four jail cells. In each you find a person you harmed, one you betrayed with full knowledge—something you did or failed to do. Maybe you hurt them physically, or was it when they weren't looking? Now you will look. Take your time. Remember. Look into their eyes. What do they say? Don't turn away until you're given your leave."

Do my friends have these things to face? Or the guys at work? I have no idea. If not, what are we doing here? No, these guys gotta know, right? Yesterday was okay . . . more than . . . I don't know now . . . too weird. Breathe! I tell myself, just breathe, and listen.

Mike

When the door opens an acrid stench overwhelms me. I can see nothing. We are bunched and moving *en masse*. I am being dragged down. I panic and grab for the wall of the cave to brace myself. It is thick with slime. My hand slips and I lose my balance. I cry out and a hand comes from behind me, takes hold of my arm from underneath while I steady myself. "It's okay," a voice next to me says. "We're going down now."

"Put your hand on my shoulder," I say, "I'll go before you." The sweat is pouring off me. I feel a hand grip my shoulder from behind and we start down. The drumming picks up.

Gradually my inner eyes adjust. I am relieved to make out stairs beneath my feet. Down we tromp at a good clip. Suddenly I have an urge to look over the edge of the railing. I pull to one side and peer over it. I can see men moving and I hear them calling out names. The distance down takes my breath away and I stagger backwards to catch myself as Buddy's voice sweeps past me: "Don't hold back, go deeper. This is your darkness and his and mine. We're going down to face the shame. If it's there, you can look at it. When you look at it, make it yours. We own it to manage it. We manage it so it doesn't manage us. This is the way we find ourselves, descending into the night. Let yourself into the shame, dirt, and secrets. Hold yourself to the light."

I am down on my knees and I am looking into the dark brown eyes of my sister, Sarah, at six years old, eyes so dark they look black. She has on her favorite dress, the plaid one with the sewn-on white pinafore. I could reach out and muss up her curly black hair. She would scream and start flailing away, trying to hit me. But I'd hold her off and she'd end up laughing. But she is crying, so I can't muss up her hair. She looks up at me and says, "Mike, I hate you." I start to cry. She keeps saying, "I hate you, Mike, I wish you were dead." She won't stop crying. I can't talk to her, I can't console her. I wish I was dead. I am crying and telling her that I am so sorry. She won't look at me now. She's turned away. The sash on her pinafore is untied and drags on the floor; it's all dirty. I want to reach through and tie it for her like she asked me to do a thousand times. I love her so much. I hurt her so bad. She has her back to me and is sobbing still. It's no use, I move on.

As Chief Seattle said: "Man does not weave the web of life, he is merely a strand in it. Whatever he does to the web, he does to himself."

Tony

Her first name is Cindy. I don't remember the last name, although we must have gone out three or four times. Maybe it was Highes. She said she was pregnant with my baby. I told her if she told anybody, I'd deny it. All she wanted was some help with an abortion and someone to talk to. She wasn't nasty about it or anything. She was Catholic, she couldn't go to her family, and she was scared, that's all. I was afraid she'd screw up everything for me. I got ugly. She dropped out of school, went back to wherever. I never saw her again. I could have a kid running around somewhere. If my wife knew this story, she would go find out.

Who can I tell that I've done this? If I tell it here what are these guys going to think? I don't know if I'm saying anything. I don't have to say anything. But I think I want to . . . I don't know. That one guy over there? He's nuts. This much I know.

I lie to my wife all the time. Not a day goes by that I don't lie about something. I can't stop it. I guess I'm just a coward about this particular thing. That and, well, if I tell her the truth, I'm pretty sure she'll leave me.

At least once a week I bring my wife to her knees. It's a rage inside me. Can be anything. The last time, I startled her and she knocked a bag of soda off the counter. One of them burst and soaked everything. It scared me for a second. Made a loud pop. I tore into her, rifled around for the grocery receipt, yelled at her for buying a bunch of shit. Told her I'd had it. She's crawlin' around on the floor trying to clean stuff up. I'm right on her heels, yelling about how useless she is and that I'm getting a divorce; and I'm getting custody of our little boy, and I will never ever let her see him. I hammer away until she's hysterical, until I've destroyed her. This is the woman I love. I love her.

A Tongue to the Tip of the Iceberg

From the moment we begin the guided imagery, we are clearing a path for the dark side, setting the scene for contact, creating a space for it to emerge. Our shame, dirt, and secrets, or SDS (its composite name), is the part of the dark self where we hold knowledge and memory of our crimes against others: the dark deeds, omissions, or desires that are in direct conflict with our values, with who we are at our best.

Instinctively we hide or deny the dark self. To do otherwise is to risk discovery, shaming, being despised, shunned, punished, and ultimately cut off from those we love or need for our survival. Under normal circumstances we certainly do not jump at the opportunity to bring this part of ourselves forward. Even more disturbing is the notion that SDS is only the tip of the iceberg, the hatch door or aperture into a much larger part of the dark self: the vast and complex badlands of the fully developed *Shadow*, the part of the dark self we hide even from ourselves.

In the initial Men's Room weekend we reserve Sunday morning for our work with shame, dirt, and secrets. In an advanced weekend we penetrate the next level of darkness, the netherworld of the shadow—a pulsating energy field of desire, fear, and knowing that exists in each of us beyond anyone's notion of right and wrong. This second journey into the dark self is what our next book is about.

Surfacing

The entire journey by guided imagery is soundless except for Buddy's voice and the drum beat. Motionless as well, for men are rooted to the spot. They may clench their fists, shift their weight, roll their heads, moan, or quiver and sweat. Some cry. But the action is all inside. Of what is seen, or heard, or felt, not a word as yet is spoken. We open our eyes at the lake once again. In silence we climb the hill and return to the heart where the men sit and write it out, of what it was, of who was there, of why and how it hurt. These are pieces for themselves, still private and inside. When this part of the journey is complete, it is time to bring the work into the heart where we give voice and witness to our darkness and the real healing begins.

To Honor and Cherish

The mission of heartwork in SDS is to break the grip of the dark self where it harbors our shame, to honor the truth and experience the relief that always follows. Our format is tight, fast-paced. If something is not clear we push for clarification but we don't linger in detail or ever ask *why,* never dwell in the ruins. Due to the nature of the work and because of the pace and intensity, many men who have resisted speaking will break out now. Each man who does this must choose to defuse his own internalized version of our universal dilemma: that our greatest desire is to be known and yet we have monumental fear of being known. It is essential to let go of the usual judgment and criticism we reserve for ourselves and others.

As leaders, our job is to create a container for the work that allows individuals to move through their fear and experience the opportunity before them. It is a moment of truth in the making for each man. The process begins at our first gathering Friday evening in "the Chapel," an old storage barn we share with an array of ancient equipment and exotic tools (every handyman's dream garage).

Enthusiastically we proclaim to the assembled (wide-eyed and terrified to darkly suspicious): "We're here for health and healing."

This happens to be the truth. Over the course of the weekend, individual men *get it,* one by one, according to their own timetable and comfort level. Some start right on Friday when it dawns in them where they are and what is possible—something that most of the men have never experienced before as an adult. Like popcorn exposed to a gradual heat-up, one by one, they pop! The others, who aren't quite there yet, stand in amazement, as if to say, "Wow, look at that guy!" As if the group were giving birth to a new species.

Then comes Sunday. About thirty minutes into SDS we

reach critical mass. Boom! the whole room turns over. Everybody gets it, everybody wants *in*. They have the courage, they want the honor, support, safety, acknowledgment. They want to stop being careful and start being human. Most of all, they are ready to express themselves directly from the heart. When this happens it is overwhelming; men choke up. All we do is get out of the way. They start to snort and gag and wheeze and sob before they get a word out.

Each of us has a story. A full story, a primal tale of a journey that has taken thirty-five or forty-five or fifty years to make and maybe forty-five more to complete. This is a big story. Even the short ones are maybe twenty-seven or twenty-eight years long to date. A lot has happened. Condensed to the cliff-hangers, boiling points, the scariest or most hilarious, the parts where you slipped off the ledge, or somebody pushed you, or you rolled somebody else off the mountain, this is good stuff. Many lessons, foibles, and failings. The frailty of human flesh. The resilience. Cowardice abounds and great strength and courage along with accidents, sickness, twists, and dead ends, beautiful creatures, lost souls, God knows what joy and sorrow.

There is a shroud we use for the dark work, a T-shirt. The background is black. On the front are two faces, one laughing, one in despair, the ancient Greek masks for comedy and tragedy, the light and the dark, like the Chinese *yang* and *yin*. As each man slips the T-shirt over his head he steps into his darkness, an injury caused. This marks the transition from keeping it private to making it public, from closed to open, from holding it alone to giving it up. The two-faced shirt reaffirms the presence of light and dark in each who speaks. In all of us, in the world, there is light and there is dark. A single tear rolls down the right side of the shirt. A man reaches for the shirt, steps into the heart, stands there, and before he gets the shirt all the way on he starts to quiver. He shakes and holds himself and he tells his story.

. . . There was a crashing thunderstorm. I took my little cousin, Amy, into my parents' bedroom, made her stand at the open window while I stripped her and fondled her genitals. No one heard her screaming . . .

. . . I try on my wife's clothing. The transformation is thrilling, as I become the woman. It's like I think Marilyn Monroe felt when her fans went wild; it's an act, it's phony, but it's me somewhere in there, going wild. Nobody knows . . .

. . . I gave her money for the abortion. Then I skipped out. She's the murderer, I thought, but it was me. Could do it. Just couldn't watch . . .

. . . She was the only woman I loved. She was exactly who I wanted to bring home to my family. I think she loved me, too. She was solid. And pretty. And smart. I didn't know women came that smart. I told her this once and she laughed so hard she wet her pants. Then she got pregnant. I blew her off . . . because why? The whole thing. The responsibility. The change. I blew it all. She got an abortion. I didn't even help. I couldn't handle it. What a loser. That was twenty years ago. Not one day goes by that I don't think about it . . .

. . . I embezzled $67,000 from my partners. Every time I hear the word "embezzle" or "theft" or "fraud," I start to throw up . . .

. . . I watch pornography in the basement where I hide it . . .

. . . I cruise the red light district and hire hookers to give me blow jobs . . .

. . . I intimidated my secretary into granting me sexual

favors. I thought it would "enhance" the relationship. It killed it. I don't even know how. All I know is I'm losing the best secretary I ever had. Mr. Big Guy, me, I'm helpless, totally powerless . . .

. . . I slept with a female colleague at a conference. It would kill my wife. It would kill her. No way I had to do that. It meant nothing. Nothing . . .

. . . fantasize about my niece. It's too much for me.

. . . I torture my father about his new wife, constantly berating her for existing and him for choosing her . . .

. . . I masturbate . . . a lot . . .

"Masturbate?" one of the men around the circle protests. "Where? In front of the Civic Center? What are you doing in the heart? Get him outta there," he grumbles, rolling his eyes. For the man who masturbates in shame, however, this is where he belongs. What grinds at the insides of one man may not bother another. Our job is to witness, to listen, to honor the man and his truth.

For many men this is their first time out of hiding, out of seclusion. It's a secret they have never told anybody, never thought they would be able to live with the consequence of telling. The nature of offenses runs the gamut . . . from child molestation to stealing, lying, cheating in a variety of situations. Most involve the big four: sex, love, money, or violence . . . always a betrayal.

Benjamin who is heterosexual was fondled by his camp counselor thirty years ago. His shame is that he enjoyed it. Others come forward who experienced the same thing or something similar.

Mark shares Benjamin's guilt.

Don recalls a homosexual experience with a male teacher as a betrayal by a man he adored and trusted, and still misses. Don is angry not ashamed. "I was twelve years old; it's normal for twelve-year-olds to have homosexual feelings," he declares.

Scott identifies himself as homosexual. "I knew I was gay when I was nine years old but I went out with women until I was thirty years old. Led them on, had sex, put myself through all kinds of contortions pretending to be what I in no way was. A lot of people were hurt because I didn't have the guts to tell the truth or live it."

Ray says, "When I was in high school, me and two friends took the kid next door down the basement and made him suck us off. He was a mess. I . . . I think . . . I keep hoping we . . . I didn't ruin his life."

The ripple through the group continues as men respond to individual pieces, express their gratitude, empathy, and even disgust . . . not for the man, but for the deed, the darkness, and for knowing what it takes for the man to stand. Men respond, "I have done what you have done." *"Who else?"* we ask. More hands are raised.

Hugh was the next to speak:

I changed the baby's diapers while he screamed at the top of his lungs. My Donny, he's a pip. I love him so much. I held and rocked and cooed at him and tickled him. Boy, he kept screaming. I warmed the milk and gave him the bottle. He only stopped to gasp for air; then he went to screaming again. I looked down at him, scooped up his tiny three-month-old body in both hands so that his underarms rested securely in the crotch of my large hands with my fingers supporting his back and my thumbs across his chest, and I shook him as hard as I could. And I didn't stop. Not for a while anyway. I thought I killed him. It's a miracle his neck didn't snap. Nobody knows. Except him, I guess. He's three years old now.

When Hugh speaks of shaking his infant son in a rage, a curtain of silence descends. It is a piece so startling and horrifying it takes the breath away, the heart sinks. Into this stillness the inner voice rises, saying: I could do that / I did that to my nephew / I know that feeling / I felt that as a child . . .

Every time one man gets in touch with his desire to harm, or with his suffering, every man gets in touch with a piece of his own. There is a voice. Not the voice of *What am I going to do now? How will it look? Am I going to be accepted? What's happening out there?* Not that one, no. It is the voice underneath that voice. It only comes to us when we are very quiet. And it says simply, "I know this man."

Jason

Now and then work will emerge in SDS that takes a little longer. The mood of the circle rises noticeably when Jason struts into the heart, like a rooster patrolling the hen coop. He circles the inside twice before he alights in the center. Pivoting, military fashion, he folds his muscular arms across his chest, but his head never stops moving as he silently surveys the group. He could be awaiting a cue for an inaugural address.

Jason is big, enviably handsome, unusually articulate. His disposition borders on arrogance but stops just this side of it so that when he speaks he comes from that place every man knows as "cool." Jason is cool. In keeping with this role, until now, he has remained slightly apart from the group —friendly, yes, confident, humorous, attentive, but *apart.* The man who would be cool must keep his own counsel. Consequently, we are all ears . . . because Cool is coming out. Cool has been quiet, but he has something to say to us now of shame, dirt, and secrets. This is gonna be good, is what the men's faces say.

"My story is about pussy," says Jason matter of factly, and we are not disappointed. He's got our attention. "I am fifty-two years old and I am an expert. For I have spent the past thirty years chasing pussy. Can't get enough of it, how about you? I married my childhood sweetheart when I was twenty-one years old. She was just nineteen—already an accomplished artist, a wonderful woman, intelligent, beautiful, talented, and in love with me. Maybe one of those . . . have you read it . . . women who love too much, I guess. Because although I loved her too, she was not enough for me. I had to have more. And because even then I was pretty good at it, I got more. Lots more. Had to have it. Just about any old place I might check into I could find a woman who could not resist and that's the way it was. You might have envied me. Many men did and many men do, but I lost my childhood sweetheart.

"This week I'm getting a divorce. Oh, not that one. This one is different. This is my fourth divorce, the second one from my second wife, who is very different from my first wife except she loved me just the same and I squandered it again, twice. Philandered and squandered. That's my claim to fame. My hero, my father, he was the same. My mother used to tell me, Don't turn out like him, don't do what he does, but I paid no attention. I did and I was. You can look in the Milwaukee phone book and find my last name. There are eighteen of us there—me and him, our wives and our children.

"I have no connection to my children, no real home, no love in my life, but I can get laid whenever I want. This pussy I'm chasing, the story of my life, is rapidly killing what's left of me. It isn't the sex that I can't do without. Maybe it's love that I cannot say yes to. My habit is to lie, to get something I need to replace what is missing, a hole in my soul where my heart ought to be or vice versa. I ply them with lies or flowers and candy. I worship at the altar of flesh. I invest in their breasts the power of Helen or Aphrodite, a Venus for my penis alone. It's a game, it's a sham, it is a lie. When they find out, love dies.

"There is no meaning to my days, I can't see long distance, only as far as tonight. The rest is bravado, all ego, all show, a habit of leaving, of coming and leaving, of emptiness spanning the years. I can't face my fear of being alone. I can't cope with tears, either hers or my own. All I know is I'm dangerous because I'm not real. There is not much of anything inside that I feel."

When Jason is finished, the group has a pallor the color of grunge. This isn't cool, this man is a sponge, a talented sponge, but sponge nonetheless. Many men wonder what would it be like to score like Don Juan or a king. If we didn't know before, we know now, thanks to Jason, who unzips without ceremony and just does his thing. The men thank him, personally, each still in awe. It's not like before but it is certainly real with gall so patently striking.

"Jason," we say to him now, "there is a place for you to begin."

Before we can name it, he shouts, "Wait, don't tell me! Let me guess. You want me to tell all the ladies the truth, right? All these women."

"That's it, that's the ticket," we affirm.

"I knew you would say that," he responds with a grin. "You want me to knock on her door with a sign that reads: I am the Pussyman and that's all that I am. If you'd like the pleasure of me in your life, stick around for the evening, after that I'll be gone." At this amusing self-portrait, he breaks into laughter, loud and clear and contagious as the truth.

What is dangerous about Jason and all of us is not our weakness but our refusal to name it. Admitting our weakness weakens it. For every man who baldly loves and leaves, there are ten thousand others who do it a little more subtly, but they do it. They use the word *love* to get what they want, they promise *forever* when they mean just today, they feign exhaustion when what they're suffering from is total lack of interest in their partners or their children. They smile and leave, smile and leave, smile and leave—living at half mast, empty of spirit, disconnected from the life they suck out of others. These are men who disappear when something is expected of them in return. Either they don't feel like giving or they don't feel at all.

This man's issue applies to us all. And the place to begin to *feel* it, is with the truth. Here is where our feelings live. Try it:

"*I feel nothing for you. But I need you.*"

Or, "*I feel nothing for you . . . but I need (*fill in the blank*: . . . sexual release, you to buy the groceries, cook dinner, bring in additional income, raise my children . . .)*"

Say it and see what happens. You may be surprised at the feelings that begin to emerge in reaction to owning the "nothing" that has protected us from feeling something.

An Unexpected Dive

Jeff anxiously kicks the toe of one shoe against the instep of the other as the last piece of work concludes. We ask him if he's alright, or does he want to comment on something? Folding one arm over the other, he hugs his own shoulders tightly and glances sideways saying, "I have a piece to do but I'm not sure if it fits?"

"It'll fit," Buddy encourages him, "go ahead."

Still, scarcely looking up, Jeff moves stiffly into the circle. He hasn't worked in the heart yet this weekend, but his presence has not gone unnoticed. He is tall and intense, forty-seven years old, a psychotherapist who discovered his vocation relatively late. "I dropped out before I dropped in," is how he puts it.

The moment he arrives in the center of the heart, he turns around and looks directly at us. There is a pause as he takes his time scanning the circle. He might change his mind, it seems, and so we are taken aback by the clarity and volume of his voice when he announces, "I feel *it* in every ounce of my body—my arms and legs, in my face, everywhere."

He does something with his face, contorts it. You see *it* biting through the jaw. There's no suppleness in the body. It's locked up—the face, the trunk, the limbs.

"Let your body express what's going on," we say to him.

He starts with the face. It looks like a spasm or tic that begins to spread by increments downward, a succession of muscles tensed rapidly one after the next until his whole body is reverberating. You could not do this voluntarily if we paid you for it. "Put sound to it," we tell him and an unearthly growl boils up from his throat.

"Arrghhhheeyehhhoooaah . . . " It starts with a "Ey ey ey eh . . . " soft staccato noise that begins deep down inside then rises to fill the room. Demonic, is what comes to mind—dark and angry, low, growlly, then rising in volume until finally it's a roar. Like a death notice. Someone is dying in grief and anger.

He is still shaking like a leaf. You can see him move into the emotions through his body. This begins the moment he arrives in the center of the circle. It takes us a bit to catch up with him. The safety of the container is holding and he has simply let go, dropped down inside himself. It's unusual. We shout to him: "Jeff, what's it about?"

"It's about my stepfather, Lester, Lester, Lester," he moans, repeating the name several times.

Jeffrey's natural father died when he was eight. His mother remarried. Whenever the mother wasn't around, the stepfather cornered him to tell him how rotten he was: "Deep down, you're rotten, kid, and you know what? You're not going to live long because of it. You're going to die like your father did . . . because you're the same kind of guy, rotten."

When Jeff tried to escape, Lester followed him, raising his voice to fever pitch threatening, "I'll break every bone in your body if you ever mention our discussions to your mother." Jeff never told his mother, not so much out of fear as his desire to protect her from more pain. The episodes continued until Jeff was sixteen and his mother divorced the man.

"I feel him in my body," Jeff hisses, "I am his hatred."

This is not anger in the normal sense. We call it *Angry,* a condition so dark inside it colors everything. It isn't about rage or having a bad temper with outbursts. It's a color inside and out, a grayish brown, the color of resentment held closely, deep down over the years, with no reprieve, well beyond the portal of shame, dirt, and secrets.

Jeff is in the circle and the thing he feels is literally moving around his body. He's able to show it to us and feel it at the same time, the shadow in the heart. We could stop the action at this point and ask him to bring the stepfather into the heart with him, to work it through further, but we don't. He is already in an altered state. He has moved through the ego, past it. The shadow, which normally inhabits the unconscious, has moved front and center. Jeff opens his mouth and out comes this demonic soul of hatred, rageful ugly bile. He is as stunned by it as we are. This is the key. Right here, right now, he gives birth to this horrible part of himself in public without shame, with no hesitancy. That's when it's over. The major piece is done.

Angry in full bloom is terrifying. When it emerges, you sense the danger instantly. The man could do harm, could lose it, rip into someone. It happens. Not here, but in real life. The container we use for the work is not the silver screen, however. No one turns and says, "He's kidding, right?" It's up in our faces, a few feet away—more than a little scary.

The work we are seeing is exceptional. We do not try to pull anything out of him. We don't really do anything except witness. In this case Jeff does it all. We witness his color changes, the emergence of the being. He just stands in the center of the heart and lets loose, lets it out . . . for every man present. When the shadow comes out, you know, we see, he can kill. This is the look. All we do is contain it, make it safe for the demon to come out.

Every Man's Angry

This unexpected dive into the darkness beneath SDS gives us a jolt. The emotional response is overwhelming. Several men are weeping for what is stirred up inside them. Each of us harbors a monster. The first thing the men want to do is get rid of it. It's like discovering you're possessed. The ego would do away with it. The ego *does* do away with it when we slip into *denial* . . . "That's not me. How could anyone do anything like that? How horrible, inhuman!"

"*Just a lover's quarrel, Officer . . .*" The man who speaks these words after he beats up his wife or lover may not be lying. We deny what we cannot bear to see. Would he go through with it if he could *be* with the outcome? This work is about "being with" the outcome in advance. His, ours, everybody's. Are we all capable of murder? We don't really know. The vast majority of us are *seepers*. We spread the *Angry* out over the years, a little bitterness here, some resentment there, sarcasm throughout. Constant criticism and judgments about others are typical attributes of the shadow of Angry.

Jeff is a psychotherapist, a healer and helper. In his mind his demeanor has to fit this Dr. Perfectly Fine persona. So here we have Mr. I'm-only-here-to-help-but-I-want-to-kill-everyone! This is the internal dialogue. The denial has to be as fierce as the *Angry* aspect of him until he's ready to invite the troll up from under the bridge. Dick Olney often urged his clients to utter the dichotomy out loud: "I aim to please, but what I really want to do is shit all over you!" Verbalizing the conflict between ego and shadow provides access to *it*, us, ourselves, that's right. "Good morning."

Managing the Shadow of Angry

We all have *Angry* in us. Those who suffer most from it are individuals who at one significant time in their lives (usually over considerable time) wanted and needed to say, "No! Fuck Off!" Instead, we had to say, "Yes, thank you very much." We *ate* it. And we continue to eat it over and over until we learn there is an alternative. Until then the inevitable overflow of internal toxins spills out around the edges of our daily lives, distorting our perceptions and putting enormous strain on our relationships, as we react to each new situation as if it were on some level the same old one—as victims.

In Jeff's case this is no longer necessary. As he moves out of *denial* and into *management,* he can turn to us (as he does) and declare: "I am one angry son of a bitch!" Finding this safe place to show the beast releases its hold on him. Will it be back? Sure. Every day. But as he practices *recognition, acceptance,* and *safe release,* his capacity to manage it grows.

It takes enormous energy to keep something this powerful submerged. When we can express our shame or anger in a place where we are honored, where in fact others benefit directly by our courage, we are washed. Each man present is anointed by the connection to the others, released from his own shroud of isolation and secrecy. Invariably a burst of energy follows, fueled primarily by the departure of fear.

Witness, Honor, Repair

The escape into darkness that many men (and women) experience as their only source of solace is the product of a world of disconnection and non-relationship. For the man who abused his sister and abuses other women, owning it is the first step. There will be more work. He will need professional help in addition to support from relationships with friends and family members. For others, breaking open the secret is enough. If a man gets in there and opens up the package, and if he is treated with dignity and love, everything changes. It is no longer Pandora's Box, it is a gift. He can open up the package, reveal the inner works, discover himself in perspective, very different.

The man who "destroys" his wife in his rage may have learned from his own father what you do to people, how you treat others when you are upset, especially those you love. Or, he may have seen his father emasculated and withdrawn in the context of his critical wife. He may have wished his father would have stood up and backed her down and now discovers he's living out that story line. A weekend with a group of men who have stories about what their fathers did to them and what they have done to their own spouses provides him with resources, the vision and the tools he needs to return to his wife and *own* his rage. Here is the starting point for moving into honor. Many of these men will be able to deal with problems they could not face before. They are prepared to find the necessary support. There is a knowing where they are going instead of being lost where they were.

Feel this resonate. Sense your darkness. Listen to it. Hear the needs within. Find someone to unroll it with. Know that what was does not always have to be. That behaviors happen when talk doesn't.

Out of the Muck

In these deeds and desires, out of the muck of the past, men discover the things that hold them apart, that isolate and divide, leaving each fearful and alone. From one perspective, our desires and behavior are dysfunctional, antisocial, even criminal. From another, they are normal. It is human. It happens. We do it, we think it. We pretend a lot that we don't, but we do. Cleansed of the burden of secrecy, connected to others, men find self-acceptance, guidance for doing it differently, and, most important, the ability to give to others.

The dark work tests the mettle. Foreboding and difficult in

the beginning, it is impossible to see in advance the good of it—the courage, grace, and strength to come. As the wolf in waiting, the hunger and fear beneath the smile, the dark self will always be with us. But there are also aspects of it vital to our creativity, sustenance, and protection. In our growing awareness we learn to acknowledge its full potential. We get a grip on it, a place to express it, get clean, make the connection. We learn how to influence the course of our darkness, a chance to use it productively for a change in our lives.

NINE

Repair Work

The Men's Room was the most positive step I ever took in my life. Without it I would not be alive today.

—Neal

■ **"My name is Barry.** I'm forty-nine years old and I have a terminal illness." The thick man on thin legs in new stone washed jeans states this proudly, as if he were showing us the latest in digital, computerized weed-pulling equipment. He has the unmistakable twinkle of someone who knows you haven't seen *this* before, even if you are not so anxious to run out and get one for yourself.

"I got the final word on it three weeks ago," he continues. "I have, my doctors estimate, eight months, outside," he concludes self-assuredly. As an afterthought, he adds, "Oh, it's a blood disease, rare, kidney related. There is no cure. On what they call the untreatable list." And he is done with it.

A hum erupts around the circle and subsides just as quickly, for Barry is simply standing there in the center of the heart, patiently waiting for . . . what? The chance to continue, or is this all he has to say? Does he expect feedback at this juncture? Why is he giving us this alarming information so calmly? What to say to a dying man who doesn't seem like he's dying?

Instinctively, we mirror his casual demeanor. No one intrudes. If he is not going to pieces, we won't either. It's a stand-off. When the room is virtually drenched in silence, Barry clears his throat loudly and resumes what is beginning to sound just a little like a Toastmaster's speech from the Twilight Zone.

"I am not, however, going to die when they say I am going to die. And I am not going to die the way they say I am going to die. I am not going to let this disease determine my death. Why should I be robbed of my dignity or get sucked into a downward spiral that leaves me totally dependent? Why should I be humiliated and degraded in this manner? Why should I take this slope down when I can choose for myself when and where and how to go down? I will be the one who decides when and where and how I will die, since it is my opportunity to do so."

"How will you do this? When and where will you die?" we ask him. For the first time since Barry walked into the heart, he hesitates. He doesn't know the answer. He shoves his large hands into his jean pockets and looks at his shoes. Then he looks at the ceiling. He starts to cry. "Whoa," he chokes on the words, stops, pulls his hands from his pockets, covers his head and face with them and begins a little dance, like a kid standing in line for the lavatory. Five steps in one direction, five steps back, all the while holding his head and by now he is sobbing.

It is all we can do to keep the other men from rushing to his aid. The instinct is to stop the pain, to abort the process because the pain becomes our own. We hold ourselves in check and he pushes himself through it. Coming to a standstill, he swallows hard, takes a deep breath and begins again. "Whoa!" he says, "I just saw it."

"What?" we ask.

"I just saw how I will die."

"Tell us," we say, and his whole demeanor changes once again. He closes his eyes, stands quietly for several moments and then, with marked enthusiasm, eyes still closed, he begins.

"It is August, August 13th, a day so clear the DJs go nuts for it. I am flying down Route One in a platinum Porsche with the top down, headed south from San Francisco on the approach to Big Sur. My Porsche is taking the curves like Sinatra does Vegas. We are in love. Me and the sky, the sky and the ocean, the ocean and the road, the road and the Porsche and me in it on fire. I am laughing. I turn the radio all the way up. I can feel everything! I'm ready. All I need is the right curve. I can remember it. It's coming up.

"A most dangerous and beautiful stretch of road, for me it's the best ever built. This is the One. The California coast. From sea level straight up into the Santa Lucias and back down again with enough edge-worn high-altitude hairpin turns to make it feel like the coast itself is spring-loaded, could just flip you out five miles over the Pacific in a heartbeat. The road is so close to the edge it falls off it regularly, just crumbles into the latest mudslide and disappears into the Pacific miles below. Months to repair and down it goes again, if not here, then there, whenever it rains enough. A vista to make you cry for no reason except it holds all the drama and spectacle and beauty that is bearable to look at in the world.

"The Porsche is opened up to 100 m.p.h., the sun is head-on in my eyes, we're over the gorge now . . . mid-bridge. I love this bridge. Here she comes, up ahead. Off the bridge, I floor it, easing the wheel ever so slightly to the right as the road prepares itself for the left-hand hairpin. I lock in. Dead ahead. The speedometer reads 150 as the gravel spews and the ground drops off.

"That's how I die. That's it. Done."

"No," we say, "Stay with it! All the way."

"Okay, okay," he yells back. "I'm over the ocean. Pink streaked blue sky everywhere. Red sun sitting on the water; Glen Gould on Bach high volume. Heaven. Whoa . . . "

Suddenly, Barry screams. "Aaaaaaahhhhhhhhhhhhhhhhhh-hhhh . . ." and falls to his knees.

"What happened?" we yell and several men rush forward to help him, but we signal them to hold back, to wait.

"I hit the water. I'm down." he croaks, "I'm under. I'm drowning, I'm gone, I'm gone. It's done."

"What does it look like?" we persist.

"Ohhhh, my God, my God," he gasps and then . . . "Oh my God!"

"What is it?"

"It's my father, my dead father . . . and Papa Gil, my grand-father. Both of them. Dad!" he calls out, "Come here! God, I'm glad to see you. I missed you. I missed you. Papa Gill, you're together! Thank God I found you. Now I'm going to be here with you. Look at me, I'm dying. I'm sick. You gotta know, I am so sick. I need you."

We pull in Dan and Douglas from the circle to give the fa-ther and grandfather physical form. And we tell Barry, open your eyes and talk to your father and grandfather directly. He doesn't skip a beat. He reaches out for the two men in a mix of anguish and joy. "I'm here. I've come to be with you now. I need you. I missed you. I'm here."

He wants to touch them, but we signal the two men to hold back. Dan, as the father, however, is overwhelmed. He's been in tears since the piece started. Out of the blue he takes over. "STOP!" he shouts.

"Barry, you must go back. It is not your time. You have a wife. You have a daughter. They need you like never before. Do you hear me? Like never before. You must go back. *You are going to get better!* It is not your time."

The room flips over. What's this? The change is spontaneous and irresistible. The grandfather picks it up: "Listen to your father. It is not your turn to die. Go back where you are needed. You are going to get better."

The men around the circle are nodding their heads. Every man nods, Yes, that's right. They take it into a chant, "It is not your time. Your family needs you now. You will get better."

Barry is confused . . . and then, as if waking from a dream and suddenly realizing it was all *just a dream,* he is elated. He lets out a whoop of joy. He rises, dragging himself out to the edge of the circle, reaching for the nearest man. Around he goes now, pumping hands, hugging men, crying, war-whooping his way along. The men war-whoop and clap him along, fully into the celebration of, well, whatever it is!

Back in the center of the heart Barry finishes up quietly telling us, "My father and grandfather worked hard, harder than many others, and they complained hardly ever, and loved me a lot and then each in his turn left me alone, and they did not say good-bye." The image is of guests invited to an extraordinary feast, who eat feverishly and depart without a word. They never acknowledged Barry's contribution to their lives, nor alluded to his responsibilities or work or family or life left over or how their departure might affect him in any way. He received no guidance, no advice, no blessing.

Grief stricken and scared to death, Barry carried on, never showing his pain. How could he? He did not know *what* to show, or *how* or *where* it might be done. Like his father and grandfather before him, he wound up all the grief and all of the fear into a tight ball and put it away deep inside of him, so that he could attend to business, to *life.*

What he was never taught is that anger, grief, and fear are

organic, not inanimate objects that can be stored on a shelf in the closet. Like all living matter, our emotions gain and lose weight. They breathe, require assistance, eat, drink, sleep. Locked up they fester. Unattended they grow long at the tooth and dangerous. All Barry could think of was how inept he must be, how cowardly to be filled with such self-pity, and how long could he go on hiding it. When he first hears of his illness, he thinks, That figures. He has come to see most of the events in his life as originating outside of himself, usually in the form of punishment.

Suicide, however grim, is the first step in a different direction, coming from the inside and moving outward. With it he picks up the reins and says, This is my horse and I'm going to ride it. But it isn't what he wants. What he wants is to return to a time when nothing is up to him. The only freedom he recognizes is when Dad does it all, or his beloved Papa Gill. So the suicide takes him back there and he gets the blessing and this leads him to the next step, the disease and what he will do with his final months on earth. Here's what actually happened.

The Rest of the Story

Barry, like most of the men, returns from the weekend elated, charged with energy. It is not the weekend but what comes next that counts. Barry comes off it with a strong positive charge and a feeling, just a feeling, that however long he lives his life is his own.

We don't know ourselves how deeply or at what point Barry learns this, nor do we know how he will use this knowledge. All we do is set the stage for it. What we do know is that when men sit down together, free of their "normal" lives and superficial identities—doctor, lawyer, Indian chief—and tell the truth of their stories, their lives, not the facts, but the impact, they leave knowing that these truths shared, these stories joined, give them control over their own destiny. Knowledge is power and this particular piece, when received, is invariably exhilarating and a never-ending surprise. We have been doing this work for more than ten years and *we* are still surprised. The process touches and fulfills a universal longing. Both of us are still moved to tears in witnessing the courage and the result, as a man reaches inside and pulls up a part of himself that has been festering for lack of attention.

Imagine it for yourself. Join the circle. There you are, wondering what can be next. This guy walks into the heart and commits suicide. Down to the last detail. He drowns. Holy mackerel, the guy has a terminal illness. (Ever thought about that? Of course!) And to escape the horror of it he is going to bump himself off. (Would you? Could you? Do you think it's right . . . for you? For anyone? Ever?) The suicide is successful, with a flourish and a splash. No? Lo and behold this man meets his dearly departed father and grandfather under the ocean. (Who knew? Did he? Would you?)

We *midwife* the event in any way that seems helpful, such as inviting two others to facilitate as father and grandfather. Right then and there something changes. These other two men have their own stories, but they know their job is to focus on Barry's story. Of course, no one walks in the door and leaves the story of his life out on the stoop with his galoshes. No. Everybody brings his story into the action, whatever it might be.

(Did you ever have a conversation with someone who actually believes he did leave his story out on the front stoop with his galoshes? He can't say anything. He can only speak in clichés and superficialities. He can talk numbers, charts, statistics, scores. But the real story is hidden. We guarantee you, whenever anyone starts telling his story, the real one, you get involved. When you find someone telling you a really boring story, you can be guaranteed it isn't the real one. This is what the work teaches us.)

Each man enters another's story at a different level, by degrees. When Dan comes in as the father, he is already deeply involved, or as we say, connected; he is already making it his own—the illness, the suicide, the father, the whole bit. He can't contain himself. "STOP! Go back!" he yells. "It is not your time. Your family needs you. You are going to get better!" So now Dan's story is in the heart along with Barry's, connected to it. It is as if these two guys who never saw each other until this weekend were writing a novel together, only it isn't fiction. We think it is fiction because we're making it up as we go along, but it isn't. Now we have a new story. And the story of every man standing witness is changed forever. *This is the magic at the heart of what we call "repair work."*

When the men begin to chant, "It is not your time!" they haven't singled out Barry. Barry singled himself out and they are chanting as much for themselves as for him. The collective response is triggered by one man's extemporaneous and compelling outburst. Who knows what might have been if we had chosen a different man than Dan to play the father? Or, perhaps we chose the right one.

Barry returns home elated, his attitude toward both his family and his illness is changed radically. He is in charge of his own destiny, he is needed, and now he is willing to serve. The resources are equal to the need, for the first time in his life. This is something to be elated about.

A week and a half later at his next scheduled doctor's appointment, the doctor takes an unusual time with the examination and tells Barry he'll call him with the results by Friday. He doesn't call. On Monday, Barry calls the doctor's office and the doctor informs him that he held on to the results to confer with "a few others" before calling. "Your tests show," he continues, "the disease is not following the usual course. I don't want to mislead you, because it could be temporary. None of us has seen anything like it, frankly, and we would prefer to err on the side of caution. Keep taking the usual medication for symptomatic relief and let's have a look at you in a month."

One, two, three months later, and it is the same story, only better each time. Two years later Barry is symptom-free, disease-free. No one knows why. That was three years ago. Every August 13th we get on the phone with him. "You still here?" we ask.

Connections There before Us

The weekend is a microcosm, a way we open the door, walk around, sample the fare. So we say again, it is not the weekend but what comes next that counts. The heart of repair work is the way in which we share with others the things in our own lives that trouble us most or bring us the greatest joy. It is moving from seeing ourselves as victims to taking responsibility, learning that the resources we need are everywhere around us if we take action to make the connection, to connect our story with the stories of others. It has to be in both directions, reciprocal, a coming together and being of service.

Many of us know how much we need. Especially do we learn how to focus on the *getting.* Our lifetime dreams are full of what we think would make us happy if only we could *get* this or that. We are not so aware of our need and power to *give,* nor how the getting is rendered meaningless if what we have to give of ourselves is never received for whatever reason.

During two Friday night check-ins we ask each man to stand and let everyone know where he is, what his body tells him, all his senses. For many men, this is a most peculiar request, for they long ago left their bodies and voices behind, while they proceed through life with their heads virtually severed from the rest of them. And the voice that issues forth from the severed head is thin, disconnected, forced, cerebral, able to produce only "appropriate" sounds. It is certainly not used for the booming, blooming truth.

So we come together as bits and pieces at first, atomized and alienated, not only from others but from ourselves. This is where the first *connections* of the weekend are made, where the first invitation is to pull ourselves together, so to speak. For some men, this is a joyful endeavor, and they take to the found voice or body in motion as bear cubs to an icy mountain stream on a hot summer day. They spy the fun in it right off. For most, however, it is uncomfortable to one degree or another.

Dan's Story

BOB ◆ On the Friday night check-in for the group that Dan and Barry find themselves in, when Dan's time comes to speak, he strides across the room. Jabbing the air an inch from my nose, he states with booming clarity: "I don't like you. I don't like the way you stand, the way you talk, the way you sound so fucking cool, the way you analyze everybody, including me. I feel judged by you, even when your mouth is shut which is not very often!" Then he turns to Buddy and says, "And you don't make me feel any better!"

Amazing. Not the first man to feel this way, but the first one to put it so succinctly, vividly, right up in the face. While the hair on my back stands straight up in response, I fall in love with the guy. We both do. The first night and he is out of the box and bucking to beat the band. Bingo, it's a connection. Mind, body, spirit, heart and all, right here, right now, the truth. And much to our chagrin, several others in the group follow suit. "Yes! Let's do it, let's tell the truth!" These guys are on a roll. ◆

What Dan is also saying is, I am afraid. I don't like being

analyzed, observed, seen, known, judged. Why is he plugged into it so tightly? Why so aware of the possibility? Because he is an analyzer and a judge. This is repair work, learning to see ourselves through what we see first and foremost in others, through our fears. It is an essential ingredient to manifesting the destiny we want rather than acquiescing to the role of the victim.

By Saturday Dan is ready for more. You can feel him beginning to build as he listens to the first four men who come into the heart to work. Off to our left, he is pacing back and forth. When the fifth man concludes his piece, Dan to steps into the heart. At 5' 11" he looks a little Paul Newman-ish with his salt-and-pepper hair and mischievous shining eyes. A flood of emotions moves through the body, up into his throat, his cheeks, and his eyes as he begins.

He tells his story in a series of vignettes, three of them. In the first he is nine years old and is sent off to summer camp. He cries for the full two months away from home. Every day.

In the second story, we catch him at age thirty-eight. He is about to separate from his wife at her request, but mutually agreed upon. He cries for three weeks straight. Every day. After four months they reunite, but he cannot shake it, the separation. He cries whenever he discusses it.

He brings us to the present in the third story. He is preparing to say good-bye to a good friend and mentor, an older man who is retiring and leaving the area. Dan is terrified that when Arthur actually leaves he's going to start crying and never stop. This is what he brings into the heart, and with that, he falls to his knees and begins to weep. It appears as if he could weep forever. Just as he is.

What has happened to this child? What ugly early loss or abandonment? But notice the way he moves swiftly through the major episodes in his life. They are close to the surface of his consciousness. There is nothing we or he must reach deep inside to discover. There it is. And the weeping continues. It's unreal. You can see the aloneness he feels, kneeling there in the center.

Every man is alone when he steps into the center but with Dan it's different. He's miles away. One gets the sense that we could all go somewhere else and he might not notice; he would simply remain alone, weeping. There is no attachment at all between him and anyone in the circle. The whole scene is oddly ethereal.

BUDDY ▼ Bob and I exchange a quick glance, a squint actually, which usually means, *I'm not sure where to go with this one, are you? If so, go for it.* Dan is still weeping softly, seemingly in another world. Bob takes in an enormous breath, exhaling slowly, before he says:

"Dan, I want you to listen for a minute here. People lose people in their lives, but they don't separate from them. They carry them along. We do this with anyone we've ever been close to—loved or unloved. We carry them with us, in our hearts or minds. If you cannot do this, the spirit connection is gone. The feeling of aloneness is overwhelming.

"You can have all kinds of people around you who love you, but if the spirit connection isn't there, you can't feel the love or their *presence* because presence is made of spirit. Indeed, love itself is made of spirit. That's what it is.

"In my experience these feelings are far more often associated with a spiritual wound than an emotional wound. It isn't so much about loving and losing as it is about being disconnected spiritually."

Who knew? I'm thinking, quite as relieved as everyone seems to be at this unexpected suggestion. Here is a man spilling out his guts, only they aren't quite his guts. We can sense the difference, but what to call it? There is almost something embarrassing about it. As soon as the words are out, they ring true. A spiritual wound.

"Do you think, Dan," Bob continues, "that you are telling us about a spiritual wound that is very deep and that began a very very long time ago?"

Dan sobs like the dike has blown. He just lets it all out now. Looking around the circle, it is evident that those of us with spiritual wounds of our own are responding, are recognizing in ourselves a different kind of anguish, and these men are beginning to cry also.

"It is true," Dan is finally able to say, "This is a spiritual wound, but what do I do with it? I'm lost with this. How can I make the connection? Can you show me how to hold someone who is lost to me?"

Bob answers: "Someone I love very much died recently. My mentor, Dick Olney. He is right behind me, over my left shoulder, especially when I need him. I ask him all kinds of questions, and usually I hear his voice quite clearly. Once, while he was still alive, he taught me a song. So this is the song I often sing when I am conjuring up Dick's presence."

This throws Dan. "I can't do that," he cries out in frustration. "I don't think anything like that will work for me. I can't hear Arthur's voice. I don't even have a song, for Christ's sake. And if I did have a song, well, I don't know . . . you're the kind of person who can sing in the middle of nothing. I'm not!"

With this, Dan slumps down on the floor and lets his chin drop against his chest. "I am useless. You're wasting your time."

"Well," Bob says, in a very deep voice. As I hear him, a spontaneous chuckle erupts from my throat. Every man snaps his head around to see what jerk could be smirking out loud at a moment like this, over this man's trouble. Even Dan stirs uncomfortably in his new-found fetal position, glancing angrily in my direction, as Bob ignores the interruption and continues.

"Well," Bob says again, "let me consult Dick on this one. Okay with you, Dan, if I consult my mentor?"

Dan casts a wary look in Bob's direction, shrugging his shoulders noncommittally.

What he doesn't know yet, doesn't yet *hear* is that Bob's voice has dropped an octave. Coming to us *live* from somewhere is Dick Olney, himself, *dead* as he is. A flood of memories surge through me, and one in particular. "Maybe we're already dead," Dick used to say straight-faced in his rich broadcaster's baritone, yet always with the hint of a twinkle in his eye. Meaning for me, not only are there many people who might as well be dead, for how lifelessly they live, but alluding also to the mystery: no one *knows* whence we came, nor where we go if anywhere. How do we know our time on earth isn't a way station between life before and whatever is beyond, if anything? How do we know we haven't died and gone to hell and this is it? Or to heaven and this is it? Isn't it always what we make of it? Dick was the master of possibility. This was his greatness. Dan is not only cut off from the possibilities, he is embarrassed by them, as each of us often is, as if it is preferable somehow to go to the grave stifled and shut down than to ever appear the fool.

"Good," says Bob, "let's see what Dick has for us."

Dan snuffles in response and nods a forlorn, yes.

"Sing Bob, sing! Dick is saying."

And Bob begins to sing (in his own voice now) and while he's singing he walks into the heart and holds out his hands to Dan, who grabs hold and allows Bob to pull him to his feet. Standing, he is wobbly and limp . . . as if he has just let go of everything; so Bob puts an arm around him to hold him steady and sort of leans Dan's head against his shoulder, all the while singing:

> *Comes now the Sun,*
> *Comes now the light,*
> *Comes now the sun,*
> *Comes now the light,*
> *Into my heart, into my heart.*

Dan is sobbing by this time. Snot is pouring out of his nose. Bob keeps right on singing. "Comes now the Sun, Comes now the Light . . ." Now, he turns Dan toward him, placing a hand on either of his shoulders. He straightens his head up. Still singing the refrain, Bob wipes away Dan's tears with his hand and he wipes off the snot from his face and brushes his soaking wet salt-and-pepper hair back from his forehead. Dan is like a little kid, a very large little kid. He is sort of rocking his head back and forth to the beat of the song, into it, wide open. And Bob says, "Now sing with me, will you Dan?" His tone is not bold or challenging, it is almost a plaintive request. A "Please sing with me, will you please?" And through his tears, Dan starts to sing with Bob:

> *Comes now the Sun,*
> *Comes now the light,*
> *Comes now the sun,*
> *Comes now the light,*
> *Into my heart, into my heart.*

What grown men will do with their whole hearts, when you just say that it's okay. Men are crying and holding each other and the circle is swaying side to side. Some are singing along with Bob and Dan, others are mouthing the words. It's like a scene out of Dickens with Scrooge holding Tiny Tim or *Brigadoon* or *Singing in the Rain* only we're a bunch of guys, a crew of strangers, castaways in a camp in Wisconsin, far from the lives that hammer away at us, drive us into the ground, far from the requisite six-pack, bottle of Merlot, toke of marijuana. We have managed to escape all on our own. It *is* beautiful. Other grown men may come along to puff and snicker, draw themselves up into a sneer, but they are only us yesterday.

Turning to Dan, Bob breaks the spell: "Dick is saying to me, Maybe Dan has a song of his own. So do you? One you could teach me?"

Through a veil of what were joyful tears, Dan looks at Bob in confusion. His smile fades, his shoulders sag as he repeats, "Song of my own?" He repeats the request dumbfounded. He folds his arms across his chest and taps his toe nervously. The swatch of wet hair falls down over his face. The rest of us stand by anxiously. Isn't it enough we are all singing? Why another song? Why does he have to have his own? Maybe someone else has one? Slowly Dan regains composure. His shoulders straighten, and we are transported to another time and place as he relates the following:

"Many years ago my wife and I took a trip to Venice. These were hard times. I had betrayed her. I was determined to win back her trust. We both knew the marriage would not last without it. I had no idea how.

"We couldn't afford the trip but I convinced her it was right. We had to start over from scratch and we had to start somewhere; she had always wanted to go to Venice, and so we did.

"The first night we booked into a beautiful hotel overlooking the Port of Venice. We were exhausted and my wife dropped quickly into a deep sleep. But I was wracked with worry and scarcely slept. Just before sunrise I awoke to the tune of a songbird amid the lightest of rains outside our wide open window. As my eyes grew accustomed to the dark I spied this fellow not three feet from my head. He was good-sized, five inches, maybe taller, with very dark plumage over his head and back, a black mask for the eyes, with a snow-white belly and a reddish tail. He had taken refuge on the covered marble floor of the sill.

"Although the curtains were billowing and a cool mist was spilling over us, I didn't move a muscle while my visitor whistled his heart out: a quick, melodious, warble ending in a short staccato beat.

"I remember thinking, What makes him sing, Why is he singing? And I laughed to myself because it was clear he was born to sing. He continued to warble away until the sun spiked the cloud barrier and off he flew into the new morning.

"I took it as an omen, you will not believe from me . . . that we are all born to sing because there is always something to sing about. And I drove my wife nuts for the rest of the trip practicing my version of his tune. In fact whenever my wife is angry at me and I want to talk but can't just yet, I whistle it up again. It never fails to bring her around . . . to make me shut up. And I will never forget the tune.

"I'll teach it to you, Bob, but you must use it cautiously. After all, this is a potent song. This is song that once won a wife back. Not many can whistle a tune like that. It goes like this . . ."

Dan whistles us the tune. It is as infectious as the tears splashing down his cheeks. Bob whistles it back. I grab my drum and a rhythm section is born. As for the rest, there isn't a dry eye in the circle, nor man without pursed lips, warbling away a little wife-winning ditty from the masked bird of Venice.

With the drum still beating in rapid short regular beats, Bob walks backward to rejoin the circle, and motions everyone to silence. When all is still he calls to Dan, "Can you hear the bird's song?"

"Yes," Dan answers.

"Now, listen to Dick's song. Can you hear it?"

"Yes," Dan shouts.

"Can you hear them both?" Bob asks.

"Yes," Dan says.

"Good," says Bob.

"Now, I want you to take a few minutes and go find Arthur and when you do, ask him if he'll join us for a little while. Bring him on in."

"Okay," says Dan, "I'll try."

Dan closes his eyes. I continue beating the drum softly. All eyes are on Dan, whose eyelids are shut but flickering. Several minutes go by.

"Where are you?" Bob asks.

"I don't know," says Dan. "I can't see anything . . . it's dark."

"Are you afraid of the dark?" Bob asks.

"No," says Dan, "I just can't see anything yet."

"Good," says Bob, "Why don't you sit down right where you are until your eyes grow accustomed to the light?"

"I can't sit down now," says Dan, "I have to find Arthur. He's in here somewhere."

"Yes," says Bob, "You're right. So perhaps if you sit down, he'll come to you. If we are always moving, it is sometimes hard for others to find us. Sit down a bit and see if he will come to you."

As if on cue, every man in the circle sits down. Bob looks up and smiles at this spontaneous show of support.

"Everyone is sitting down now, Dan. We're all waiting for Arthur." With this Bob stops talking and the drum beat picks up volume. All eyes are on Dan, eyes still closed, who has started to move his head around in circles, as if to stretch his neck muscles. Soon every man in the circle is starting to stretch his neck muscles.

"He's in," Dan says suddenly breaking the silence, but his voice is barely audible.

"What did he say?" the men are asking each other while straining to hear.

"Where?" says Bob.

"Here," shouts Dan, pointing behind his right shoulder.

"And what does your mentor, Arthur, have to say to you?" Bob asks.

"I can't tell you," Dan says.

"Why not?" Bob asks, clearly disappointed.

"It's very personal," says Dan.

"Oh, c'mon," says Bob. "We're here to get personal."

"I love you," says Dan.

"Really?" says Bob, "Thank you. I love you, too."

"No no no," says Dan, opening his eyes and looking at Bob with irritation. "I mean that's what Arthur is saying to me."

"Ohhhh, I get it," says Bob, "That's great!"

"Can you bring in Marian?" Bob urges him on, "Now find your wife."

"Sure," says Dan, quite casually as he shuts his eyes, folds his arms across his chest and takes a deep breath. "Whoops," he quickly adds. "I'm sorry she's too busy right now."

"Oh, please," says Bob, "Tell her it is important."

"Nope," says Dan, "She's busy!" he insists. "We have to wait a little bit now. Marian hates to rush. She says I always rush things. Wait, here she comes. Bob, it's her!"

"Where?" asks Bob.

Dan points out to his left, about two feet in front of him.

"What is she saying, Dan?"

Dan unfolds his arms. A smile moves across his face until he is beaming and he booms out: "I TRUST YOU!"

"Good," says Bob. "Please thank Arthur and Marian for visiting us. Tell them, they are welcome anytime. But before they leave, why don't you tell all of us what your intention is now?"

After a moment's reflection, Dan proclaims: "I will maintain the connection." ▼

Bringing It All Back Home

> *When I walked through the door that evening, Nancy clearly saw the difference in me. I do not know what that looked like, but I know that I felt a lightness in my being, as if a thousand-pound weight had been lifted from my shoulders.*
>
> — *Norm*

Repair work, as busy and everyday as it sounds and *is*, is the goal of the Men's Room experience. It starts the moment men arrive for the weekend, actually before the weekend. The real beginning is the decision to come, the act of registering, committing oneself to at least explore a new course of action, wholly unknown, reputed to help . . . but who knows? This takes courage. It exposes a need, and with it a little bit of the truth is out and the process is underway.

By the time they leave, if nothing else, men want the truth in their lives and usually they want a lot more. They leave with a vision, a microcosm, a tiny sample of experience that they will need to replicate in many other forms again and again in a world that is often unsafe, if not downright hostile.

For repair we provide the place. There is a swatch of time, made up of the lives of the men moving through it. It has a color, a texture, a feeling and a healing way different from what has come before and what will come afterward. We move among each other in such a way as to stitch it up, repair some of the torn places, heal some of the damage done to the web of our lives.

We can also tear it up, rip it open, let the night air in, moving among one another. This is not all a fuzzy harmonious enterprise, although there is an abundance of laughter and warmth, all essential to health and healing. Repair work goes on all the time actually, with no beginning, no ending, like housekeeping, life-keeping; but like keeping up anything, it gets low-down messy from time to time.

At the root, repair is about making and utilizing the connections between our lives and others', especially acknowledging the damage or wounds we have sustained, for the purpose of moving out of the pain and back into life. It always involves connecting the body and mind, heart to head, exhuming the injured spirit. It means rediscovering the inner voice, telling the truth, and bringing our stories front and center to join with those of other men.

In so doing we acknowledge the pain of our initial wounds without shame, and we allow the victim in each of us to come into the light. In order to heal we must experience genuine acceptance in an environment created to incubate and sustain an entirely new sense of self, where we can welcome help from others, discover a nurturing father within and outside of us, and meet and assume the authority of the responsible self. Ultimately, we experience repair in learning to give with total generosity. We get there by developing the ability to manage the victim inside, taking full responsibility for our lives, and discovering that the resources are equal to the task we lay down for ourselves, as well as those coming from left field or on high.

TEN

I Will

In Mayan culture the men climbed 365 stairs to the top of the pyramid. Here they knelt before the high priest for his blessing. Each one kneeling and then rising would make his personal proclamation. If he did not speak the truth, the priest quickly dispensed the transgressor over the edge to his death.

■ **Wilson is** forty-five years old, 6' 3", 195 pounds of rock'm-sock'm fighter pilot. His appearance in all aspects is tight, so that for an instant we have before us a hammer in search of a nail. He strides into the heart, pulls the T-shirt over his head and gets right to the point: "I'm out here because of my anger, which mainly I take out on my wife. It's explosive. I tear into her verbally. I am ashamed of it. My intention is to control it."

We ask him to name the kind of anger he feels. Is it a

direct response to feeling hurt or an outburst that is out of control, a rage? Does he use it to maintain control, to stop his wife from gaining control over him, or does he use it as punishment, to hurt and intimidate her into subservience?

Wilson reflects on this and answers, "I would say it is to control and punish her, I'm not sure why . . ." He drifts for a moment and then adds: "I am controlling and punishing." Now he is finished. He has done it. He has owned it publicly and he is ready to walk off. But we ask him to stay in the heart.

Crossing the Rubicon from the edge of the circle into the heart is a major voyage, but sometimes not far enough. Chomping at the bit or in lagging anguish they come, they talk. But in order for a man to take the truth home with him he needs to bundle it in a vivid encompassing image, one he can remember long after this group, rapt with attention, has dissolved. The image must come from the man's story. Wilson presses further into his own. He speaks of his childhood and finally returns again to his wife: "I need to annihilate her. I can do this directly or I can go after the kids. I can't get out of the rage until she cracks."

The rage has nothing to do with her. It is all about him. He uses her to get it out of his system. For the first time he is going to be able to tell her what he knows about his anger, which goes way back. With this understanding he can ask for her help. He will need her help in order to give up the control and the pleasure (fleeting relief) he experiences when she "cracks," like he once did at the hands of his father.

With this image, cracking and opening, to annihilate the pain, to let it out, let it go, he is ready to get clean. He wants it. He has always needed it, but he could not see his way through to it for the shame, for feeling it was too horrible, too humiliating to own. It is difficult, there is usually some humiliation in the owning and it takes courage to give up the bit of control he has walled around his wound over the years. Yet the greatest emotion he will have in giving it up is genuine relief. Then comes the reward, immeasurable in its effect on his relationship with his wife and their life together. Now his proclamation has teeth:

"I will own my rage to my wife," he declares unequivocally.

This leg of the journey is about commitment, setting the reclaimed self into motion. In the beginning the men look at the proclamation as the conclusion of their work. In fact, it is the beginning, step number one (364 to go) to the top of the pyramid.

Wanting Despair

It is pitch black on Friday night. A crackling fire illuminates the cavernous shell of wreckage we call the Chapel, where thirty-nine of us sit in a circle in hushed anticipation. We ask the men if there is something lost or missing in their lives right now. And if they could find it over the course of the weekend, what would it be? Without hesitating, John speaks out, "I am lost in despair. What I need to find is hope."

The next time we hear from him is late Saturday night. Fifteen men have been through the heart. It has been a long, emotionally charged day with much good work behind us.

John trudges into the heart and begins speaking in a low confessional monotone as if he really does not want us to hear, much less respond. "I am in a deep hole of despair," he starts where he left off the night before, dropping his chin to his chest as if bowing slightly. Straight up he would probably reach to 5' 10", but the translation before us is about 5' 6".

The story that follows is endless and dull, like a single key on the piano played over and over. A yawn ripples around the circle until it seems all will be fast asleep and snoring soon. Even John may fall asleep. His eyes are half closed, nestled in their sockets over two half-moon pouches of crinkly gray flesh. He is not fat. If we could plug our ears, he would appear trim. He might be handsome if he had a smile and his eyes were open . . . you really can't tell.

There is no musculature in his cheek or jaw line. Although he is sober, the words spill out of the lazy mouth of a guzzled second martini. It is his wife, his life, his work. Nothing is going right. This is the way it is, has been, will be. As he drones on, his head bobs listlessly back and forth across slumped shoulders. "No one can help, there is nothing to be done," he concludes without punctuation. A broken record of despair. Deadly.

Revving up the scene, we ask him point blank. "Where are you, John?"

Clearly, John is not in the room. In fact, by now, several men have checked out and are just now rousing themselves . . . from whatever reverie.

"I'm in a hole, I said!" John says, raising the volume, as if we hadn't heard him.

"Tell us about the hole, John," we snap back.

"Fine, good," John perks up a bit, "It's got eight-foot walls. It is very dark. It is a dirt hole and I am at the bottom of it."

This is workable. We go with the hole. Thirty-seven men arrange themselves in a human wall around him, standing barefoot, three deep, arms and legs interlocking, and facing outward, away from the circle. John, also barefoot, is in the center alone. Locked in. As the human wall is completed, John's energy level rises. It is an impressive hole. This seems to suit John. The two of us outside the wall can see his head bobbing up and down in the center. He's saying, "Good, you guys got it! This is it. This feels like the hole I'm in. Perfect."

He's animated. This is good. The bad news is that he likes it here. You can see his eyeballs peeking out through the shoulders. He is smiling.

"Get down on all fours!" Bob shouts to him, "So you can feel how deep the hole is."

Down he goes. The hole swallows him up. We can hardly

hear him at this point. The voice is muffled, but unmistakably enthusiastic. At this point, as the men will later recall to him, everyone is annoyed with the charade. It is late. They are exhausted. Several guys are ready to pop him one, especially hearing him go on about what a swell hole it is. If we had said, "Okay, now everyone turn around and spit on him," there wouldn't have been a dry mouth in the house. The men are thinking, Doesn't this idiot want to get out? Is he just going to settle in for the picnic or what? What a wimp!

The air fills with exasperation and contempt. Every man here has been in the hole. They have no tolerance for it. They cannot stand to see anybody in it, let alone enjoy it. As one man put it, "I was thinking, Go ahead and stay there forever, you little piece of shit. You'll never get out!" The other part is that these guys think he can't get out. On the one hand they want to torture him for being there. But they also doubt he can make it out. This is adding to their distaste.

It is time to work him. "You ready to stay there all night?" we ask.

"Nope," he says. "I gotta get outta here pretty soon."

"Okay," we shout, "Whenever you're ready."

"Okay," John shouts back, "I'm ready!"

Silence all the way around. We say nothing. Everybody waits. Pretty soon John repeats, "Okay, I'm ready now." No one responds. Obviously, he expects the wall to dissolve. Nobody moves. More silence. Then in a whiny cajoling voice, John declares once again, "Okay, I'm ready. I said I'm ready."

"Are you sure you're ready?" Buddy calls to him.

"Yes!" John shouts. "Right now!"

"Well, then, do it!" Bob shouts back, "Right now."

"Wait a minute," John calls thoroughly annoyed. "I can't get out until these guys let me."

"Too bad!" One of the guys shouts back . . . unable to restrain himself.

"These are not guys," we say to John, "This is a hole. If you want to get out, you have to get out."

John leaps to his feet and urgently tries to pry a couple guys apart . . . but no go. There is no hole in the hole.

"Look," we call to him, "if you want to stay in the hole, stay there, but if you want to get out, get out. Quit fooling around!"

Silence. He says nothing. He stands erect in the center with his arms crossed across his chest looking indignant. He will wait it out. We all wait. Finally, he says, "Fine, have it your way. I'll stay here," and plunks down in the middle of the hole, cross-legged, elbows propped on knees, with his chin resting in his cupped hands, the five-year-old in a complete pout. And he sits. The silence descends again . . . this time for a very long time. It is the kind of silence before the first shot is fired in battle, thick and merciless in that there is only one way out now.

Soon he will start begging, we begin to think, when suddenly, instantaneously—in ten years we have seen nothing like it—John rises up. Nobody sees him coming. One moment he's down in the hole and the next he's perched literally on the backs and shoulders of four guys. He flashes a mouthful of teeth at us as he springs over the front row of men and lands like a cat on the floor outside the circle. Astounding. The wall dissolves in confusion. One man gets out a "Whoa!" John faces everyone, looking somewhat surprised himself . . . as well as a little cocky.

"I'm out!" he declares, "What's the big deal, anyway?" he adds in an off-hand boast.

The muscles in his face are working, his eyes are open. He is alive. "The big deal," we tell him, "is that when you were in, you looked like a seventeen-year-old house cat with no wind left. Down for the count. Now you look wild. Like a bobcat!" He beams back at us. Doesn't say a word. Doesn't have to.

We tell the men to spread out, all the way to the walls. "Give this man room." Turning to John we say, "Okay, show us the bobcat again!" And with this he sweeps across the floor doing cartwheels, spinning, leaping like a gymnast. He's all over the place, crouching springing, growling, snarling, screeching as he flies through the air. Incredible. The guys are smiling and as John continues, the smiles spill into laughter. Still he does not stop. He keeps leaping around. Now the men start cheering, hollering and throwing high fives to each other.

He is definitely out of the hole. And he has managed to get all of us out of the hole late on this Saturday night. The transformation is beguiling. He finishes and stands in the center of the circle, looking ten, twelve years younger, wide awake, full of himself. And handsome! Despair vanquished. Shame dispelled.

John himself calls the circle back to order. Scarcely able to speak for breathing so hard, he stammers, "This is what is missing . . . missing from my marriage, missing from my job. This is what is missing from my life."

"What is your proclamation then?" we ask him.

"I will keep my wild cat alive," he declares, "I will bring him home to my wife, I will take him into my work. I will keep my wild cat alive!"

"When you start to slink back into the hole, notice it," we caution him. "Probably before the weekend is done, you will start to sink again. Be aware. Use your wild cat, practice with him, keep him in your heart."

Out of the Glare

First, the man comes out of hiding because there is nowhere to hide. There are only places to cower and snarl at the miserable or impossible or difficult or confusing hands we are dealt—all the reasons we list for why things are not as we would have them, all the shortcomings (ours and others), the bad luck or sour buck, and oh the many failings that are not of our own making, that we have inherited. This is what we leave behind when we come out of hiding, and with it the reactive, avoidant behavior that only brings us more of the same disappointment. It isn't magic. The bad news does not disappear. The process is more like flipping the rearview mirror to its dim setting, so that you are not blinded by the glare of what is behind you. You can focus on what is in front of you.

What allows us to let go of the past is forgiving our trespassers and foregoing the comfy reassurance we once gained from our own despair, self-flagellation, vivid recollection of deeds done to us or by us that we need to remember only as they serve to guide us to higher ground, sweeter days, a world unstuck, and then turning with an open view of the road ahead. Easier said than done, but the proclamation is rudder, is there made of heart and muscle to hold and remind us where we have been, where we are going.

Simon Says

Simon lumbers into the heart sobbing unabashedly, his huge torso lurches toward the center like a wounded bear. He can't put on the T-shirt. Out of the question. So he fastens it crudely around his neck. "A shroud in honor of my beloved grandmother, who passed away fourteen years ago," he announces, beating his chest with clenched fist. Now with arms outstretched he throws back his head as if to invoke the presence of the Almighty in the confession that follows.

From yesterday's heartwork we know the theme of abandonment has wrapped his life in grief equal to the mountain of flesh we see before us. Two fathers disappeared, one through divorce, the second through death. His physician warns him that he is next in line. Yet he persists in eating his way methodically toward this ready grave. His wife and two children beseech him to consider their fate without him.

Now, during SDS, he speaks of a betrayal many years ago of his beloved grandmother. Raised without father by two women at war with one another—his mother and his father's mother—as object of their contention and love, he has never known peace. He lived with his mother and loved her very much; but the grandmother was his soul mate, and when he was old enough he stole every spare moment to run to her side. This aggravated his mother further and the jealousy between the two women was lively right up to his wedding day, when it looked at last as if he might escape the turmoil.

"When the date was set," he told us, "I sat down with my mother and I said to her, Grandma is going to be there. My mother answered, If your grandmother is at your wedding, I won't be."

No one in the family could figure out how to have it happen. In the end, Simon forbade his grandmother from attending.

Now he cries out: "Why didn't I tell my mother, She's coming and you're coming and that's it. It's my wedding! Why couldn't I do that? All my life I've let others decide for me. All my life I've not stood up for myself. And then the worst happened. While my wife and I were on our honeymoon, grandma died.

"Every month for fourteen, fifteen years I go to the grave site. Every month I come back from it, feeling just as bad. I listen for my grandmother's voice for guidance, for forgiveness, for anything, but it doesn't come. I cannot continue without her in my life."

We signal one of he men to come behind Simon and become his grandmother. Meanwhile Simon has continued to apologize to her. Now we tell Simon that his grandmother has something to say to him. Once again we become amazed at the wisdom residing in all men.

Chris, speaking for grandma, says, "Simon, you must stop apologizing. You only apologize because you want people to accept and love you. Be honest with me. Tell me what really happened and I will accept you."

Simon, through sobs, can be heard to say, "I didn't tell your daughter, my mother, that I wanted you there. I didn't tell her how much it meant to me."

Grandma responds, "Then you must go to your mother and tell her what you did not do. But there is something more important, Simon. You must make a proclamation to be honest, direct, and truthful with people for the rest of your life. And most important, my grandson, you must live with the truth about your self. You must face what you have done to your physical self. You must be honest and know that you've been killing yourself, slowly, from shame. You must stop. Your children will be lost without you. They and your wife love your loving, dear self. Be honest with your self and take care of your self."

Through sobs, Simon proclaims, "I will stand up for myself and the first leg of this journey will be for my health and the well-being of my family so that I do not abandon them as I have been abandoned." We suggest that he dedicate the entire journey to the memory of his grandmother. In response, Simon shouts, "I dedicate this journey to my grandmother, and I will keep to it until I can get into this T-shirt!"

TANA

After the weekend Simon drives two other men back to the city. They come to a stop sign but it is not the usual 4-way stop he was expecting. Simon is speaking excitedly about his grandmother and the dedication of his life to health. "Please God," he declares, "don't let me die before I can fulfill this promise!"

He stops at the stop sign, steps on the gas, starts across the intersection. The man in the back seat suddenly screams, "STOP!" There are cars coming at them from both directions full speed. Simon throws the car in reverse, slams down on

the gas pedal, the car screeches into reverse; he slams his foot
on the brake and the car comes to a halt, barely tapping the
car directly behind that is just arriving at the intersection. He
might have smashed into it . . . but no, just a tap. No crash,
no damage. So he turns to the other two guys in the car and
says, "I guess God is going to let me do this after all. TANA!"

In The Men's Room we say, "There Are No Accidents:
TANA!" For those of us raised strictly within the conscripts of
rational western humanism, this phrase sounds nonsensical.
"What do you mean?" they may ask or complain. "There are
accidents every day. My whole life is an accident!"

"Happening right now," we are quick to add.

When we view our lives as accidental, we tend to see ourselves as victims. We hesitate to initiate, to intervene, to
change direction. The nature of accidents is that they are out
of our hands, out of control. No one is responsible.

If, on the other hand, we shift our perspective to greet our
circumstances as part of a plan of our own design, our focus
shifts too. We are free to discover and create our own role.
Who are we in this scene? How can we be? What do we
want? The veracity of the teaching is academic. In practice it
simply means what happens next is up to us. We ascribe to
TANA because it promotes responsibility. In the proclamation, I Will . . . we create an intention whose core is of honesty, integrity, responsibility, not anyone's but our own.
When the vision (image) and action required are combined,
change occurs from the inside out and our relationships
evolve accordingly. No accident.

Tap Tap Tap

Marlon is a tough guy, a contractor by trade, physically imposing, confident . . . "a bit of a perfectionist with the rage of
Hades burning inside of me." This is what he's in for. Rage. It
comes out at home, work, play . . . wherever. Something
snaps, he loses it, he lashes out. It is always overkill. In the

aftermath he is filled with shame until he can restore his defenses and convince himself that he is surrounded by idiots, that it is not him, but them. His work is respected, but he has a bad reputation for being "impatient, overbearing, and particular to the point of unfairness. I am not what they call a good team player."

From heartwork done earlier we know that Marlon had a very critical father. So his own rage is not surprising. What goes around comes around, often scarcely modified from one generation to the next. In the heart for the second time he spills out his guts, owns his rage and self-contempt, and completes the piece with a solid intention to manage his rage.

At this point, Bob stops him, saying: "Sorry, I don't buy it."

With this, Marlon's eyes bug open. His demeanor of sadness switches to outrage. "What are you talking about? I get up here and tell the God-awful truth and you say, No, I don't think so . . . Who the hell are you?"

The man is done. He got ready, he pushed through to it and now he is done. He wants nothing more than to slink off and lick his wounds. Humiliation compounded . . . we want him to stay in the heart.

BUDDY ▼ "I don't know," Bob picks it up. "Something is not right here. There is something else going on. Let's just stay with it a while. Okay Marlon?"

The expression recedes from Marlon's face. Mr. Tough Guy, Mr. Do-what-is-required-and-do-it-better-than-most, is off balance. He looks lost. Watching him, I cannot tell what he is feeling at all now. We have seen him move from declaration, confession on the verge of tears, then outrage at being challenged, and now it is as if an unseen hand plucked him up by the hair and shook the bejesus out of him so all the emotion has swooshed out the bottoms of his feet into a puddle on the ground. There he stands stock still now, pale and blank before us, as if he might be sinking slowly into shock. If I reached over to touch him, he would feel clammy. Clammy and drained, is what it looks like.

Again, Bob intervenes, "I don't think you have to deal with your rage."

Marlon stares at him blankly, mouth loose and open slightly. Finally, he responds, "Well what the fuck is it?"

This isn't said with rancor. Rather, there is a kind of sunken quality, sunken and bewildered. So, maybe it isn't rage. But what is it, if not rage? The rage is a cover. Best defense, strong offense.

We are all prone to glom onto cover emotions figuring (often unconsciously) if it worked before, it will work again. What we need to ask are questions like Am I really mad, or do I actually feel guilty? If time allows, one can usually wind on down to what is underneath. It is easy to miss this trick we pull. Emotions are like fuel. We use them to maneuver around obstacles without really showing much of anything about what is going on underneath. Most men are experts at this, or rather, men are practiced at masking any emotion, whereas many women can fly quickly from one to the next like a honeybee through the garden until they're sucking on something that suits the moment. Sometimes we assume women are closer to their true emotions, but it is not necessarily so.

In any case, Marlon is still rooted to the spot, looking cadaverous, when Bob intervenes again: "What I am looking at is an egg," Bob says, "a beautiful egg with this incredibly thin shell, so thin in fact, I can see through it. You might think about owning how incredibly thin the shell on your egg is. You may need to see for yourself that it is so thin that when you are approached by anyone who comes up and taps on it—tap tap tap—it scares you. It could break. If you can own your thin shell, how fragile you feel, then you might experience the rage differently."

Privately, I ask Bob how he zoomed in on this with Marlon, and he says, "How the fuck do I know?" which is just Bob's I'm-a-man-among-men-in-the-woods way of saying that we communicate with one another all the time on levels indiscernible to the naked eye, unspeakable by the tongue. (Eventually, in a more formal setting, Bob adds, "It is in the style of *how* he gets angry. As Marlon talks about his anger, you can see the sadness in his eyes. They are the eyes of a scared boy, not the eyes of a murderous man. It isn't rage. It's the panic.") ▼

Now we see the emotion in Marlon pick up. His color comes back. He is not altogether convinced, but he is curious and tempted. It could be better to be sensitive than out of control. He sees that. Now he wants to change the intention to going home and telling his wife, "Stop tapping on my shell! Stop being critical of me!"

We interrupt, "This is not about telling Kathy or anyone else to stop tapping on your shell. In this work you say what you feel. If your wife taps on your shell, what happens to you?"

"I am afraid. I get scared," he answers. "But it isn't so much the tapping itself as how she does it," he adds. "She comes at me."

"What is your intention then?" we ask.

"Okay, I will tell her how it feels inside my body . . . that I am afraid. I panic. My heart races. I feel like I'm losing it, losing all control. I will tell her it feels like she is going to hurt me."

With this intention, focusing as it should, first on his relationship with his wife, Marlon will find out more about his own fears and also what he needs from her. In this proclamation he is getting the idea that regardless of how she (or anyone) treats him, he will get further with the truth, with a direct, accurate expression of what he experiences (that usually sends him into a protective rage). This is the wellspring of change, how relationships that are stuck begin to turn again.

Workable proclamations must involve those we are close to right now. Timing is very important, striking at the highest point of motivation. There is a precision of intent, purpose, focus, muscle, and heart. Like the young Mayan warrior, you can't fake it, because the truth is self-evident. It doesn't work unless it is the truth. We don't ask for a blessing based on falsehood. There are many routes over the edge and down under . . . of which the Mayan example is perhaps merely quicker and more merciful.

Four Ways We Proclaim

The mechanics are easy: stating in a positive manner what you are capable of and willing to do. I will make the phone call. I will join the 12-step. I will own my rage. I will leave the office at 6 P.M. For those who are perpetrators of abuse it means developing new kinds of connections with those we have harmed, concrete ways to be of service to them in a way that balances our past destructive actions.

Each man repeats his intention four times, to the four directions. Borrowing from our Inca predecessors, we begin facing the South, the land of the snake where the past is shed like an old skin to reveal what is new and vital. Turning clockwise, we proclaim to the West, where we face fear, the setting sun at the end of the day, the black panther and death. Now to the North where the elders reside, where wisdom is, each man makes his proclamation. And finally we proclaim to the East where daybreak catches the eagle in flight, where the sun rises and new life begins. With each turn the intention grows in certainty as each man honors the past, acknowledges his fear, marks the wisdom of the elders, and then turns to give birth to himself anew, right now, with this I WILL.

A substantial proclamation is the result of an arduous journey that always involves a degree of anxiety and stress. We expect it, we accept it, we commit to move through it. It comes as a release from the bondage of our injury. Workable proclamations focus on addition, not subtraction, balance, not erasure. We don't change who we are but how we deal with who we are, which enables who we can become. Effective proclamations are made publicly and kept public, to honor, engage, and strengthen our connections to one another and to community. Proclamations unfold over time as they become a part of one's life's work. What each of us needs to do, we need to do again. And again, onward into an honorable life.

ELEVEN

Honor

Yes, your Honor . . . (your honor? or my honor?) I swear to tell . . . (Oh my God, now I've done it, I've got to speak it, not just know it) the truth . . . (What's that? What's the Truth anyway? We all see things differently) the whole truth . . . (Can't even cut a guy a little slack, can they?) and, nothing but the truth . . . (sure, but could I do this forever?) so help me God (yes, God, help me . . . please someone help me!).

The Shame of Judgment

Donald comes to the heart. It's late Sunday morning. He knows time is running out. The routine is clear. Come into the heart, put on the T-shirt, and get it out. Donald's not clear. Perhaps he has never been clear. Now, he's nervous, pacing back and forth. He's wired, anxious, throbbing.

Head down, still pacing, he says: "I judged every one of you in this room. I couldn't relate to any of you. I saw all of you as beneath me. If you came into my office in a suit, I'd relate to you . . . I'd know we were on the same plane. I'd still judge you, but we'd be level, the rules would be clear. But here, from the get-go, Friday at the fire . . . ever since then, I judged you all to be sick—all of you. This was the wrong place for me. I shouldn't have come here. I couldn't relate to anything you did or said. To be honest, I judged every one of you as a loser or a nut case. Every one but Buddy. And he's okay only because he came to my office in a suit and talked my kind of talk about my company. He wore a suit, a tie. He fit in. My kind of guy. I knew he was okay. But if people aren't dressed in business mode, I don't trust them at all. I judge them, all of you, to be inferior. And, talking about wounds from the past, crying, showing any emotion, you're definitely not people I'd hang out with."

It all comes back now. We've been checking in on him since Friday night. He felt he didn't fit. Thought about leaving but wouldn't let Buddy down. All the while thinking This is unreal, I don't belong here. At Saturday's mid-day break we take the men down to an open field. We have a basketball, a football, and a softball. Sports brings back incredible memories for the men—good ones, bad ones.

Donald was a good athlete, still is, and, in case we didn't notice, he spends lots of energy evaluating how bad everybody else is. This one can't catch, that one can't throw, who taught you to dribble, *ad nauseam*. At the end of an hour we've taught them to do a lay-up, how to run a pass pattern and throw or catch a pass, and get a softball caught without breaking their fingers. Then we take the group to the edge of the field, where it adjoins the lake. We have them elect someone who can represent all of them and their collective feelings about athletics. He will do something on behalf of all of them. They are to put all of the shame and negative feelings about sports—about dropping a key fly ball, about being excluded from teams, about being taunted for having butterfingers, being the strike-out king, being sent to the Siberia of right field, all of it—into that ball. And, this one man is going to heave this ball into the lake to rid all of us of this judgment and shame.

This was the moment Donald knew he couldn't escape. He was the child who teased, taunted, shamed all the others. Nothing has changed. He's still doing it, shaming people constantly. Either you compete at his level or get out of the way. Now, he's in his own path. Thirty men were ridding themselves of what he and others like him had done to them. It didn't miss him. He tried to contain it. Do what he'd always done, try to move forward, through it. But it was working its way through him. Up and out on Sunday.

Donald has stepped up and owned his judge. "You guys don't judge. I JUDGE. I judge the way you judge. I am THE judge. It's been this way my whole life. I thought it was good. In my family we never really talked to each other, certainly not like here, or like you guys say you want. In my home you looked good, did it right, or you were teased mercilessly. But mostly, when we talked, we talked about someone else and how weird they were. Relatives, friends, neighbors, public figures, everyone came under our magnifying glass and one or the other of us ridiculed them. If they had a flaw, we found it and turned them into road kill."

Judgment is part of all families. Us versus Them. It's part of work and life. Comparisons. Few come out on top. Mostly it brings us down. For Donald, it was a way to stay on top.

We ask him to pick one man in the room whom he has judged and bring that man into the heart. He says; "I've judged all of you . . . I could pick anybody . . . it doesn't matter." We let him know that it does matter. He needs to slow down, look them each in the eye, and pick someone who has been a repeater, someone who has not been so easily dispatched with a flick of his sword. He brings Gene to the heart.

Opposites Attract

Gene has been a deeply expressive, emotional man. Every-man's work brings Gene to tears—wracked in tears—needing to be held, comforted. An ocean of emotion. Every piece of work has tapped into what seems like a bottomless lake of sadness and empathy. In ancient Greece, men saved their tears in cups and it was a sign of great manhood to have a full cup. Gene's was overflowing.

Donald starts in immediately. "I couldn't get past you. I couldn't figure you out. Every time someone said something, you'd bust out crying. First I thought, Get a grip, guy. Then I figured you were a nut case or a weakling, an off-the-wall wuss. Then I start seeing that you're not weak, you're a good athlete, strong. I didn't get where these tears were coming from. I still don't get it. They make me nervous, but I kinda admire you. You really feel things and you let them show. I think it takes a lot of guts to let your guts hang out. I'm afraid to do that. I judged you to be less than me, but I think I may be less than you. Wow, my dad would have a field day with this! But, I'd like to learn from you . . . maybe not get as good at it as you . . . but learn how to be with my sadness."

Donald has noticed his judge, owned it, and taken a step toward managing it. He is moving into Honor. This is a way of life. It is about having nothing to defend and no one to defend against. Some would say it is our toughest battle, the battle within the self. It is the battle to be impeccably honest with yourself and be willing to share that with others. It requires us to know the big and the little commitments and contracts we make every day—and live up to them. Or, to know when we've slipped, as we surely will, and be honest about that. By listening to our bodies, we know when honor is with us and when it has slipped away. It takes very little to have the openness and expansiveness of honor be replaced by the shortened breath, tightened muscles, and collapsed, protective sense of being out of honor. Slick, dishonest, tactical, or conveniently self-serving are the ways out of honor. The life we live presents us with many temptations. Some of them will lead us off the honorable path and on to treacherous terrain.

A life of honor moves us beyond self and honesty. Service to others elevates us into honor. Emotional and psychological support top the list. You can start now with those closest to you. Beyond that you can build, carry, mentor, do for others in your community. Do not look for reciprocity. Give freely and the honor expands. Honesty and generosity of spirit with self and others gives life purpose, meaning. It heals the early wounds to our self-concept, our spirit.

When we give without needing something in return, we receive immeasurably more than what we gave. We are responsible shepherds of all our relationships, not victims of them. We are in charge of what we put into them, what we add to others. What we add helps determine what we receive. There is a balance in the world of relationships. But, we never stand still at the balance point. It is made of shifting ground and we must learn to move and shift with it or be buried by it.

Pulled in Two Directions

Vic is a thirty-eight-year-old real estate speculator. He makes Type A look like it's written in lower case. He's over-committed, plugged into phones and beepers, has a computer with him in his Mercedes when he arrives late on Friday night. He's so overbooked, working on several deals, we should be glad he made it at all. Work is an avalanche he's skiing over. His adrenaline rush keeps him just beyond the crush of it all.

He'd really like to use the phone, check on a deal, smoke a bit, share a couple of business stories, about being leveraged 35 to 1 and coming out way ahead, but we're into this emotion stuff. It's outside of his comfort zone. Can't make a deal with it, no vision of an upside. On the way to dinner Saturday night he pulls Buddy over. "I'm going to have to leave. There's a big deal we're working on. The meeting's scheduled for 8 A.M. tomorrow (Sunday). I'm pivotal to the deal—gotta be there." Buddy confronts his decision to leave. Buddy loses. Vic is set on leaving.

Buddy tells him that he needs to be in Honor when he leaves. He needs to come into the heart and explain why he's leaving and say Good-bye. It's a way of honoring his commitment to be there and being in relationship with the others in an honorable way. Vic agrees.

After dinner, back in the heart, there is no Vic. He has skipped without a word. Buddy does the explanation, creates the closure to let us move forward. The shadow of Vic is gone, but his ghost lingers. The work is a little tougher this night.

Sunday morning rolls around. After breakfast we're in the heart preparing for SDS (Shame, Dirt, and Secrets) when Vic shows up. He's right into the center. "Last night I knew I couldn't face you guys. You were all so into this. I was struggling with it. Business deals were everywhere. I drove home, kissed my wife, and went to my office. I was on the phone from 10 P.M. till 1 A.M. I made some stuff happen so I didn't need to be at the meeting this morning, I knew that I needed to be here . . . to do this work. Caught a couple hours of sleep, kissed my wife, and now I'm back. I just didn't feel right leaving. You guys cared about me, not how many bucks I had in my pocket. You guys have showed me a side of life that I've been running from. It's a side of life my wife has tried to get me to slow down for, for years. I'd just go put another deal on the fire, no time then for her or this. When I was driving home, I felt it. I felt myself closing down, becoming smaller, tighter, ready to do the deal at any cost. I realized that I was leaving a part of myself behind. I needed to get back here, to thank you. Your heartwork reached me. I care about you even though I hardly know you . . . no, actually, I know you better than anybody else that I know and that's why I had to come back. I don't want to run away from knowing people. Driving back here, I realized that I've got to listen to my wife's feelings, get to know her too, care about her, want to be with her. I've got a lot of work to do."

Don't Look the Other Way

In what ways do we harm others, or ourselves? Lying, cheating, stealing, being irresponsible, inconsiderate, withholding—big and little actions and avoidances to save, protect, contain, and control a situation so we don't have to face ourselves and our neglect, inadequacy, failure, or injury. If you've lived, you've done some of this. You can recall the energy it takes to carry these things inside. You may recall not looking people directly in the eye, looking away, feeling loaded down and heavy. You may have found yourself defending a statement with excessive energy or shifting topics to evade the truth. And yet, in the moment of the truth, we always hear people say; "I feel so much lighter. It's such a relief to finally have it out."

So, what do we not see, not want to see, that remains hidden from our awareness? How are we shaming or discrediting others in our lives? We slash people with our verbal stilettos and then turn away denying and avoiding the damage we've done. This work embraces getting closer to knowing these parts of ourself, the parts that take us out of honor. Anger, unrelenting teasing, shameful exposure of others—these are what we slip on and cause our fall from honor.

Many of us live lives of dishonor with mates. Often it's a result of being too attached to our mothers. Frank is a man like this. When we met Frank, the outside world would have said he was "squeaky clean." He was seen as honorable, admirable, highly successful, and a leading researcher in his field. He always had time for civic and other matters. Everything, that is, but his wife. In many ways, she did not exist for him. After all, she didn't do what Mom had done for him. She didn't applaud his every move. She wasn't there to send him off to work with a prepared lunch. She refused to be in the background. In fact, she demanded time and attention, occasionally interfering with his concentration on data.

Two Women

While Frank was young, his Mom had turned to him to be what her husband could not be for her. Frank was to become someone she could talk to, listen to, be proud of, be inspired by—someone who would always be there for her. When Frank married Pam, he was caught between two women. Subtly, he sought out Mom's support whenever things got tough with Pam. He came down on decisions in ways his Mom would support. Pam struggled to have Frank talk and negotiate things with her. Frank would listen to her and then do what he wanted. Once, he disappeared from her sickbed in the emergency room to return to his writing because he figured "the doctors will take care of her." Over their fifteen years together he had abandoned her physically and emotionally, holding on to his connection to and support from his mother.

At the weekend, he discovered the chains, the umbilical cord that still connected him to his mother. He saw his manipulations of Pam, the ways he frustrated and cut off her attempts to create a stronger fabric of a relationship. Now he needed to do something about this. It could not be from weakness, from capitulating, begging, crying, or in any way trying to get from Pam what he'd gotten from Mom. Frank needed to engage her in an honorable way. He needed to own his awareness with strength and commitment. He needed to begin dealing honestly with his mother as a man and with his wife as a husband. And, all of this would have to be built up moment by moment.

Turning a life around does not occur instantly. The insight alone about the dishonorable nature of our lives doesn't change anything. What has to happen is the building, step by step, moment by moment, of a new life that's based in that kind of honesty. It's a life that lets people know what the limits are and what the truth is.

Coming Home

Quiet Brett left The Men's Room with the others Sunday at 1:30 P.M. A two-hour, silent ride home in front of him. At forty-eight years old, he'd had a lot of demons to dig up, confront, and grow beyond on the weekend. He'd seen how despite his anger at his dad's walled-off feelings, he'd done exactly the same thing to his wife and children. He'd been moved by others' work and had, perhaps for the first time, felt deeply his own sadness, anger, and isolation. His work really began in the car. What would he tell his wife, his children? Should he just say it was a great weekend and see if anything was really different tomorrow? Or, could he come clean? Do this strange thing called "being in honor"? It is such clumsy language, and how would he do it anyway? Two hours debating the issue. Changing his mind. Rehearsing how to set it up so he could come out okay, not lose the respect of Lannie and the girls.

Brett could see the house as he rounded the curve into the *cul-de-sac* and onto his driveway. His mouth was dry, his heart was up into his throat, and suddenly he was face to face with Lannie. Those eyes—expectant, tears in the corners, now flowing down. Fumbling for words, he said, "Let's go to the yard. We can sit on the swing." Then, out there, he said, "Please sit on my lap, I need to be held." Now they were both crying, and Brett was able to enter his work: to speak in honor of his silence, of his father, and of how he knew he'd injured his wife, his children and, painfully, himself. He knew he needed more time with the men to practice. He knew practice was the goal because he couldn't possibly achieve the level of closeness he wanted now. But he knew that he didn't want to return to the silence and the lost time.

Months later, for Father's Day, his daughter, whom he had also talked with, sent him a card. Inside she wrote: "I saw this fall scene, the rustic setting, and could smell the woods and thought of where you were when you had your weekend with the men. I wanted to let you know that it meant so much to me to hear you acknowledge my strength and your appreciation of my ability to express my feelings. I am so thankful that you can recognize who I am, acknowledge it, and verbalize it, too. I know that you see it because you've begun to see it in you. Your involvement with The Men's Room and your new friends has really empowered, opened, nurtured, enlightened, and lightened you. It's wonderful and I applaud you. I plan to follow in your footsteps. You are a hero to me—one I now know I can count on."

Together in Honor

Catholics, for centuries, have used the confessional. Jews have a day of atonement, on which they say aloud the sins they have committed over the past year. Every culture asks its people privately or publicly to come into a place of honor.

The stress of living in today's competitive, high-pressured life brings people out of honor. It challenges our ability to hold to the high ground. First in little ways, later in larger ways, we move out of honor, honesty, integrity. We slip from omission to commission. At The Men's Room, men see their mis-steps, their fallen ways. They identify the demons and ghosts of dishonor who eat at their table. They struggle with them, they learn to manage them. They even learn from them. Then, they must ceremonially leave them and engage with a new path—a path with heart. This is the path of honor.

Walking this path, revealing previously hidden parts of

ourselves to someone important, notice not only your own body sensations. Also pay attention to what's happening to the other person. You are not alone in the world. They are responding. Their color, muscle tone, pupil dilation, breathing are all mirrors that reveal who they are and how you are being received. At the weekend, men feast on the immediacy of response.

When they leave the weekend, sadness fills the air. They have become close, caring, and open with men. It's a first. They have become born to their fathers, brothers, sons, and comrades in this journey. The heart has been a womb. They've gone through a gestation and now are emerging into that other reality. There is talk about how to keep this going, how to bring it into their homes and offices. But they will trip, fall, stumble. Some will get hurt. Others in their lives will not be ready for who they now wish to become. Others will be ready but doubt what they see. They may be tested to prove someone else's belief that change cannot have happened. They are scared and in need of each other's support. They can get that with calls, lunches, and bi-monthly leaderless meetings. But largely they are on their own for ninety days, armed only with shifts, proclamations, honor, the wisdom of their bodies, and a flood of experience.

In this ninety days they must hold to their path or they will find the ghosts and demons back at their table. They write a letter to themselves that they get several weeks later. It spells out their path, sometimes in great detail, sometimes simply. Warren put it simply:

In the last forty-two hours I have walked on the same path with thirty-six other men. They are very close to me as I write this in my $55 seat on the edge of the heart. I have begun much work. I have made friends—there's a new word. We've all made proclamations. Mine is to manage my rage, my anger every day. I choose to bring love and friendship *into my family and life. I pray my friends and I stay this course.*

Ninety days later, Warren prepares to attend our reunion. On the windshield of his car is a note from his wife along with a Native American rattle.

Ninety days ago you opened a whole new world of possibilities when you went to The Men's Room. I want to congratulate you on the hard inner work you have done. Some days I can't believe the change in you. I know you are working hard to control the rage that lives in you. You are doing great! Keep doing it every day like you promised yourself—you bring honor to your self with each step you take.

I fell in love with you the day we met. I can't imagine life without you. You are a terrific father, friend, lover, and husband. I don't think I could be luckier. The work you've done has made a difference in our relationship. As unbelievable as it seems, it just keeps getting better. You have touched my life, my heart like no other person—forever—just as I know you touch the lives of those thirty-six other men on your journey.

This rattle is for you. You may share it with others, but it is a gift from my heart to yours. Shake it with love, joy, pain, frustration, whatever you need it for. Let it remind you of The Men's Room and every step you take on this path.

If I could go back in time, I'd pick a father like you for me. I'm so glad Ricky and Ellen have you. Keep up the heartwork—dreams really do come true.

TWELVE

Amen

■ **Our time** together always ends in a circle. The circle symbolizes our growth together. It is the Native American spirit-catcher capturing good energy. It is our mandala, a healing circle possessing all that has entered it on the weekend. It is a representation of individuals becoming a community. Each man's movement from incredible isolation into healing contact is felt as we look from one to the next. A weaving has begun. Across the circle lines of relationship, experience, shared history, struggle, survival, and emergence are woven. The gospel song "Amen" reverently blossoms from the group.

It was something like a first love—The Men's Room—the one we never forget, with all the tentative moves, filled with uncertainty and hope and expectations of something unnamed. I came without a ghost of a notion of how to be close to another person, how to be with men in any but heady

*ways. Filled with questions, not the least of which was: Am
I gay if my leg touches another man's as we ride the train?
How to be available to my children? How to allow my wife
to get near me? All, while shouldering the mother lode of
pressures heaped on mountains of fear. I didn't have a friend
or know how to be a friend, so I went looking for one, because life was too difficult without a friend . . .* (Gary)

While singing, the men have an opportunity to go inside
and inventory the blessings that have come to them during
the course of the weekend. Commitments they made, relationships they've begun, renewed focus on those awaiting
their arrival all building inside. Outside themselves, the
eyes, heart, and spirit of each man stands in ready support,
encouragement, and love of them. They will not be left.
They will not leave.

*I was so scared I almost didn't walk in. All those men
seemed to belong and I knew I didn't. I hoped, with a lump
in my throat, that one of those guys would be my friend.
Worse, I hoped that no one would notice the shake in my
voice or my sweaty, cold fingers and the tremble in my
hands. Man, this was a time I needed a friend.*

   *Ten years later we are still meeting and I love these men. I
love them with more passion than I could have ever
dreamed. They have trusted me and I them. We have become family. We tell each other our deep truths—both the
dark and the light. We support, we comfort, we listen with
depth and caring. We fight and challenge one another with
love.*

   *What I have learned with them is that all that really
matters is love. There is only love and the fear of not having
love and all the craziness that comes with that fear. So, The
Men's Room was a new beginning—find my self, my true
inner strength of heart; learn to be open, stay open; honor*

my truth and be there to help others into their truth . . .
(Albert)

Hopefully, as you have read through this book, you have
paused, reflected on your own history, your story, your development. Perhaps shifts and blocks have come to mind. We
hope you've been comforted by the camaraderie of other's
efforts to lift themselves out of isolated and destructive patterns. Commitments and proclamations may have come to
mind. People whom you wish to get closer to and the actual
distance that exists in those relationships may be clearer
now. We are blessed with the capacity to impact the world
about us. Coming out of isolation into relationship and community are healing steps.

We must start with one awareness to share with one
friend. This begins the process of discovering that we're not
alone. We must build on this with time, experience, consis-
tency, remembering what was talked of, returning to it with
renewed interest or deepened awareness. Men can help each
other stay focused, go deep, feel accepted, reach out to those
they fear or depend on. Men can support one another in
their committed intimate relationships to try again, to do it
differently, to be honest about self. Together, men can assist
others younger or older, bringing them hope and healing
their community. We can father a new era—one in which we
guide, model, demonstrate, teach, nurture, heal, encourage,
invest, energize, coach, strengthen, risk, shepherd, and stew-
ard an honorable and responsible, conversant and accepting
male image.

We know that men need to learn from each other in ways
that their fathers could never model. Men need to know that
their stories are both unique and no different from another's.
Kent wrote to us:

I was stunned by what I saw and heard: men who, with the

aid of sensitive, insightful and deft (but not always delicate) facilitation, were able to lay out their hearts and insides for all to see and hear, sharing what they had kept hidden, even from themselves, for most of their lives; men I felt were so despairing I feared they were only the merest emotional self-nudge away from doing themselves final, ultimate harm; men who were so palpably full of suppressed anger that violence seemed their next action of choice. I saw them talk of their shame and self-blame and suffering, shout out their anger and heartbreak, and then, with the participation of their fellow men present, find varying degrees of relief and the beginnings of healing.

For me it was a series of one-after-another experiences that found me empathically aligning my own being with theirs, and seeing myself in every single one of my "brothers." They helped me to the realization that none of us, whatever our background, experience, or ancestry, is all that different from any other one of us. At the level of the heart, we all suffer and celebrate the same human feelings. I now dig deeply to feel deeply.

As we conclude, we wish to share the words of men who have found this community and begun to birth this new male model. With the words of men who have been through the weekend, we wish to convey to you the blessing of being fully alive and deeply passionate about your life. This will place you on a path, a journey—at times slippery and dangerous—to examine, challenge, and honestly communicate that life to others. They in turn will share theirs with you. Four letters—about healing wife, son, father relationships—capture the drive toward open relationship that once stimulated seeks ever higher levels of involvement.

I came there feeling no joy in my life. I was bitter and unhappy. Things always seemed to be happening to me, not by me. I always got the short end of the stick. Little or nothing worked out for the best. And, the only emotion which I seemed to be in touch with was anger—actually, rage.

When I broke out of the shackles of this existence during the weekend, I began to cry like I cannot remember crying in my lifetime. It was from a deep place within me. My entire body was weeping. What a wonderful release. I was delivered into a new life, one with color and feeling.

What came with it was the recognition of how my prior actions had harmed people in my life. Most of all my wife. In the closing circle of men, I felt a deep sadness and understanding wash over me. I had tortured her, made her the object of my pain, my problems, my disappointments.

I knew then and there that I would have to change. I would appreciate a woman who had loved and lived with me despite six years of venting my pain. I would make it up to her somehow.

When I walked through the door that evening, my wife saw the difference in me. I do not know what that looked like, but I know that I felt a lightness in my being, as if a thousand-pound weight had been lifted from my shoulders. I felt an indescribable freedom that was unlike any other time in my life that I could remember. I knew that I was now free to give of myself in my marriage . . . to show her how much I loved and appreciated her. My life has changed forever. I've derailed a downward spiral and begun my life again, begun my marriage again. (Nick)

Jeff checked prior to the weekend to be sure footballs would not be part of it. We assured him that there would be one there, but it would be dealt with without competition or shame. After the weekend Jeff wrote:

I grew up without a father, fat and very bad at sports. I spent a great deal of time avoiding these activities all my life.

When my boys got to be interested in sports, I always went to their events. Yet, I always found a reason not to throw the ball with them—I know they noticed, I know it bothered them. But no one had ever taught me and I was too ashamed to show this to them.

I faced this and more on the weekend. I was taught not only how to throw the ball, but how to talk about fifty years of not throwing or catching it. I told my sons after the weekend. The next evening there was a box on my pillow. The football inside had a note attached. "Dad, it's never too late. Love, Craig."

We throw it back and forth every now and again. I do it without shame. We have fun. We share about the times we didn't—how that was for both of us. And, I've given a gift back—my son will attend the next weekend. There will be more for us to toss back and forth.

Trent concluded his heart work with the proclamation to be a responsible son. At twenty-nine years of age, his work had opened up the depth of emotion that had been blocked—his grief, rage, and hunger for connection with his mother and father, broken twenty-five years ago in a divorce.

I set the goal of becoming more deeply connected to the people in my life . . . dialoguing about personally meaningful issues. I needed to know and be known. My journey involved creating a safe place for myself and others to share and explore with me.

I called my father. I asked if we could sit and talk quietly about our relationship. He responded positively and with warmth. I had taken the step of being direct and deliberate in a relationship. My father is an extremely rageful person. An aloof person, he never really let the women or children in his life into his heart. He did not know how. I now know he desired to do so. I know this because he is very willing to engage with me on matters of the heart. The difference is that I can now help him do what he could not do for me. I can ask. I can make myself a presence in his life. I can hold firm to what I want him to hear and what I need to hear.

I am very proud now to be my father's son. For a time, my rage clouded that pride and I did not actively love my father. I did not show love for any of the men in my life until the weekend. The rage is not gone. I recognize that it will always be a part of me. But it will not own my life. It will not determine the nature of my relationships. The shell of denial that was once the only safe haven, hangs looser, tattered by months of facing the pain, feeling the support and joining the process of bonding with other men who made themselves available. (Trent)

Frequently events occur at the weekend that are beyond explanation. A kind of blessed magic works its way into the fabric of the weekend. Tom came knowing that a thousand miles away his father lay ill. Saturday had been powerfully focused on father-son work. Tom was deeply moved. Late Saturday night he received a call. His father was dying. He flew to his bedside. Before leaving, he taped a message to all the other men thanking them for their work, their support, and expressing his emotions as he prepared to be with his father in his last moments. He said that he would need and bring all our energy and love with him. In the heart, Sunday morning, twenty-four men spoke their deepest feelings into another tape to be sent to Tom. They spoke of their own losses, of their love for him and their commitment to be there for him upon his return, of the many emotions that a moment like this stirs up. Later, Tom wrote:

I made some enduring friendships on that weekend. There have been times when I'm not sure where I would have turned without them. Less obvious is the way the weekend allowed me to be available to my father as he began to die. It is no accident that I missed the last half-day in order to be with my father as he lay dying. Or that the energy I needed to be present came on a cassette from all of the men in my weekend. The new awareness of my own feelings generated by the weekend allowed me to honor my father and myself at the last moment. TANA!

Arm in arm we stand in that circle. We feel the spirit of mankind and it is about kindness. No man is superior to another. No one is in the center. No one is more powerful, more worthy, more or less important. The circle's strength is based on being joined—rising and falling with each other. It is our son-shine. The circle, the sun, our brotherhood goes back to Mayan, Inca, Hopi, Greek, Italian, Chinese, and other cultures. Throughout history, in art and literature, men have healed each other's injuries—physical and emotional. Gathered around together, speaking late into the night, performing ritual and ceremony, their spirit renewed.

Blake needed the weekend. He was in the midst of a major life crisis. It shook the foundations of his life. An ethical, moral person, he was wrongly accused of a transgression. Others, inflamed by their own righteous indignation, were suing him. He felt like he was "in a deep dark hole holding on to the edge for dear life." He had become very depressed and struggled to find the energy to live his life. He couldn't manage this crisis on his own. Like many men, asking for help was the final straw. As Blake put it:

At the core of my being, I felt deep shame, anger, and sadness. Having grown up in an alcoholic family, I had been carrying these feelings for many years. To get free I had to return to the beginning. I needed to do more than "talk from my head" about my feelings. I had to locate them in my body, speak them, move them, move me, move on.

I went to the weekend numb and terrified. I had buried the shame, rage, and sadness of my life growing up in an alcoholic family. I had to bury them to survive. And now, my life was full of them—past and present. Seeing my father drunk every day had made me want to kill him as a teen-ager. I hated him. I hated myself. Now I was spreading shame around for my family as he had for his.

I faced these buried emotions as well as their all too real, current brothers. The other men gave me courage. I remem-ber how supported I felt when I was able to own and express feelings of shame in my life. I sobbed. Bob came over and said, "I understand . . . I can see you now . . . You'll be all right." He smiled and gave me a hug. For me, this affirma-tion was tremendously healing. I get warm, positive feelings just remembering the experience.

Three years later, the legal questions were resolved favor-ably. Our continuing men's group was celebrating its third anniversary. I brought in five pounds of legal documents that symbolized my shame, anger, and sadness over three years.

I asked the other men to lay pillows on my back and then lay on top of me. I felt their weight like a ton of bricks. I struggled to breathe. I had the feeling I might suffocate and die. I began to grieve the deep heavy shame from the black hole inside of me. I grieved so I could live released from the shackles that had bound me these past years.

Afterwards, I burned the symbols of my shame in the out-door grill. I stood with my friends in a cold, drenching down-pour as the blue and orange fire burned into dark ashes. This was not yet enough of a purge.

I became naked and with my friends' help, rubbed the ashes of shame, fear, and sadness into my skin. Some of them joined me. Like the warrior who eats the heart of his enemy for strength, I had embraced the darkness of my life and become more alive than ever before.

Though my sister and brother-in-law greeted me with a strange look when I arrived home, face covered in ashes (they were our house guests), my loving wife looked up as I entered the bedroom, smiled warmly, saw the look on my face, and said, "Welcome home, you've been away a long time. It's good to have you back."

From more than a decade of work with more than a thousand men, there is no doubt left in our minds that men crave deep, meaningful contact. Of course, we love to talk work, politics, and sports. Releasing the pressures from the straight-jacket of work is a priority. Yet, in each man we have met, from a variety of life and socio-economic situations, we have witnessed a deep reservoir of feeling in search of a way out. What has amazed us is the swiftness and quality of the emotional roller-coaster ride these men will take together. The mood can go from anxious anticipation to deeply moving sadness that permeates the room and then flips into riotous laughter that fills the heart. The men learn to go deep, yet not wallow. They learn that catharsis is not enough. In fact, that it can be dangerously addictive. It can draw us down into repeated bursts of emotion, resolving nothing. Instead, we must move forward through our fear into healthy interactions.

The men who have gone through the weekend know that they must get a vision of the kind of relationships they want to have. They know that they are responsible for the quality of those interactions. They know that they must focus their intent, their full presence, on that vision to make it happen. With the role models and experiences they integrate from the weekend they develop a picture of the future. This future image is a magnet. Hopefully, its charge is strong enough to draw them and you forward toward it. Stronger, in fact, than the charge of the past which has kept them from heartfelt contact.

To hold our vision lined up in the lens of our intent or resolve—knowing what we *will* do, not try to do—requires the challenging, non-shaming support of others. By now, we hope you are ready to share, or have already shared your memories, responses, insights, fears, hopes with others to begin the building of your circle, spirit-catcher, or community. This journey has many steps. For Allen,

The Men's Room is just a beginning, where loving men part the weeds so that I may see my path and take the steps I need to take to listen, to be generous, to be patient, to forgive, to know what I want and ask for it. I see it now as the threshold to an existence of connectedness that is now my life. This feels sacred to me. I feel something I'd call God present in those moments of deep honest connection.

When vision and intent hold steady and true long enough, relationships with significant others take on new qualities. Greg let us know of how this worked for him:

Life with my wife has been the most special change in the past eight years. My work with the men and with her has changed our relationship into a loving, respectful, honest, direct, safe, and fun partnership. She has truly become my best friend and lover after thirty-four years of marriage.

Ben and others have experienced this as a catalyst, a way to expand their limited world view. Ben wrote to us about the concentric circles of change he has seen. It has been a bit like dropping a stone in the center of a still pond and watching the ripples flow to the edge:

The change nearest my heart is with my family. I can accept the love and kindness of my children with a measure of humility. I tell my wife of my deepening appreciation of her

and witness our relationship improve. My contacts with my mother and father are less encumbered by confusion and resentment. My sisters and I speak freely and feel safer with one another. Five years of history with men from my weekend has put us through the crucible of a broad range of life's circumstances and we stand strong with each other—challenging and supportive. Professionally, as a doctor treating infectious and terminally ill patients, I have developed a warm, spiritual holding of them beyond their illness. I'm able to speak more clearly about issues surrounding death without having my own fears contaminate those conversations. I embrace my physical and spiritual community. I find that small shifts in my consciousness can lead to dramatic changes. I wish I had the ability to write some nifty conclusion, but in the end, I'm a work in progress. I await the changes to come.

Many men's faces are before us now. They have so generously offered their own life experience for us to learn how to work with others. Now, you have these experiences and models to take you forward. No words can thank them enough. The real thanks comes from growing the size of a circle of men committed to a caring future. If you share your inner experiences with friends and family, listen to their reactions and experiences. Take a step toward deepening those relationships. When you do this you will honor yourself and the men whose lives we've presented here. We must hold ourselves accountable for what happens in our lives, in our communities. Sharing ourselves with loved ones, shepherding others, contributing with our time, our spirit, our mentorship to those we do not know, these behaviors will heal our wounds and take the community of humankind a positive step forward—one we do not take alone—on our evolutionary journey. So . . .

It's as if you will remember me as your

teacher who pointed the way but now you walk

on this path with your own two feet ~

And you will find your sense of joining hands

and walking into the deep river

growing more and more clear ~

The great integrating principle of the

unconscious will reveal more and more meanings,

one inside the other, like a nest of Chinese boxes ~

And you will be clearly guided by a

sense of awe for the great river into which

you venture and a sense of reverence for all life ~

DICK OLNEY
MAY 31, 1915 – OCTOBER 3, 1994